EXILE

"This fascinating and deeply moving journey to the edges of the Jewish world tells a story of heroism and perseverance that enriches our understanding of contemporary Jewish identity. One wonders how much longer these communities will be able to endure, and that open question only makes this book all the more poignant and urgent."

—Yossi Klein Halevi, Senior Fellow, Shalom Hartman Institute

"An intimate and engaging tour d'horizon of the diaspora, *Exile* is an essential resource for anyone seeking to understand contemporary Jewish life outside of Israel and the United States. Annika Hernroth-Rothstein has written a remarkable book and performed a crucial service for the Jewish people everywhere."

—Michael Oren, former Israeli Ambassador to the United States, Author of the *New York Times* bestselling *Power, Faith and Fantasy* and *Six Days of War: June 1967 and the Making of the Modern Middle East*

"Too long considered merely a problem to solve, the Jewish diaspora isn't an abstraction but, as Annika Hernroth-Rothstein reminds us in this important book, a gorgeous mosaic of rich traditions and complicated circumstances. Like the best observers of the human condition, she weaves together sweeping historical narratives and tender everyday moments to show us how Jews from Iran to Finland succeed in preserving both the shared and timeless memory of our people and the diversity of experience that makes our ancient religion eternally vibrant. It's time we toured the vast and lively Jewish world out there, and we can ask for no better guide on this journey than Hernroth-Rothstein."

—Liel Leibovitz, Senior Writer, *Tablet Magazine*, Co-Host of the *Unorthodox* podcast

"Western observers often characterize Judaism as a religion, though this is far from the whole story. For at least 2000 years, the Jewish Family has embraced a wide diversity of belief - and non-belief. *Exile* introduces this family's disparate branches, visiting them in their ancestral homes in North Africa, Central Asia, the Middle East, Latin America, and Europe, and lovingly telling their stories."

—Tal Keinan, Author of *God Is in the Crowd: Twenty-First-Century Judaism*

PORTRAITS OF THE JEWISH DIASPORA

ANNIKA HERNROTH-ROTHSTEIN

EDITED BY TIFFANY GABBAY

BOMBARDIER
BOOKS

A BOMBARDIER BOOKS BOOK
An Imprint of Post Hill Press

Exile:
Portraits of the Jewish Diaspora
© 2020 by Annika Hernroth-Rothstein
All Rights Reserved

ISBN: 978-1-64293-187-7
ISBN (eBook): 978-1-64293-188-4

Cover design by Cody Corcoran
Interior design and composition by Greg Johnson, Textbook Perfect

This is a work of nonfiction. All people, locations, events, and situations are portrayed to the best of the author's memory.

Post Hill Press
New York • Nashville
posthillpress.com

Published in the United States of America

For Theodor and Charlie
My greatest blessings and my true north

CONTENTS

Jewish Glossary

Alef Bet The Hebrew alphabet.

Bar Mitzvah [Bat Mitzvah] The term applied to a Jewish boy [girl] who has reached the age of thirteen [twelve], indicating that he/she is considered an adult in the eyes of Jewish law and therefore responsible for following all laws and commandments of Jewish observance (the term literally means "son [daughter] of the commandments").

Brit Milah The ceremony in which a Jewish boy is circumcised. The Brit Milah (or Bris) takes place on the eighth day of a boy's life.

Bubbe, Zayde The Yiddish words for grandmother and grandfather.

Chanukah Literally, "dedication" in Hebrew. The winter holiday commemorating the rededication of the Temple in Jerusalem after a group of Jewish warriors called the Hasmoneans defeated the Syrians who had defiled the temple and attempted to force the Jews to assimilate. Also spelled Hanukkah.

Chevra Kadisha Jewish burial society/undertaker, responsible for preparing and sitting with the dead before burial.

Chutzpah Audacity and/or extreme self-confidence.

Daven To pray.

Diaspora/Galut Diaspora means "dispersion" and Galut means "exile." Both words signify Jews living outside of the Land of Israel, away from a vibrant Jewish community; Galut is also used to describe the time period since the destruction of the Second Temple at Jerusalem.

Erev Literally, "evening" in Hebrew. When placed before the name of a Jewish holiday, it means the day before the evening that begins the holiday (since days in the Jewish calendar begin at sundown, Jewish holidays begin in the evening).

Goy/Goyim Hebrew and Yiddish term for a non-Jewish person/persons; meaning "gentile."

Hareidi/Charedi Ultra-orthodox Judaism.

Havdalah Literally "separation." The ceremony that marks the end of the Sabbath on Saturday evening.

Hechsher A rabbinic stamp of approval designating a product as kosher.

Hevruta A study partner (usually applies to study of Torah in a yeshiva).

Kabbalat Shabbat Special prayers and songs included as part of Friday night services to welcome in Shabbat.

Kibbutz An Israeli cooperative village.

Kittel A robe that is worn by religious Jews on Yom Kippur, when leading High Holiday services, when leading a Passover seder, by grooms at weddings, and as a burial shroud.

Kosher Derived from the Hebrew word "kasher," which means "proper" or "pure." Most commonly used to describe the dietary law of the Old Testament or Torah, it can be used as a term for something that is proper and good.

Maariv Evening prayers.

Machzor A Jewish prayer book for the High Holy Days.

Megillah Literally "scroll" in Hebrew. There are several books in the Jewish bible referred to as "scrolls," but when used by itself, this term usually refers to the Scroll of Esther, which is read on Purim.

Mensch Literally meaning "person" or "man" in German and Yiddish but has come to mean "person of integrity and honor."

Meshuge Yiddish word meaning "crazy."

Mezuzah Literally, "doorpost" in Hebrew. Refers to a small rectangular box or other container, found on a doorpost in a Jewish household, which holds a parchment containing several passages from the Torah.

Mincha Afternoon prayers.

Mitzvah Literally means "commandment" and can also mean good deed.

Moreh [Morah] Hebrew for a man [or woman] teacher.

Pesach The Hebrew name for the holiday of Passover.

Purim A holiday, celebrated a month before Passover, commemorating the victory of the Jews over the evil Haman who sought to slay the Jews of ancient Persia.

Rabbi A teacher of Torah, derived from "Rav" meaning "great one" and "Rabi," meaning "my master."

Rebbetzin The Rabbi's wife and/or a female religious teacher.

Rosh Hashana The Jewish New Year.

Saba, Savta The Hebrew words for grandfather and grandmother.

Shabbat The Jewish Sabbath, which begins at shortly before sundown on Friday night and ends about forty minutes after sundown on Saturday.

Shacharit Morning prayers.

Shalom Literally means "Peace," commonly used as a greeting between Jews.

Shema A prayer recited in most Jewish services, as well as at bedtime and when death is imminent; one of the most important and well-known prayers in Judaism.

Shikse A non-Jewish woman.

Shiur A lesson on any Torah topic, such as Misnah, Gemara, Halacha, and so on.

Shtetl A town or village with Jewish inhabitants, commonly found in Eastern Europe before World War II.

Siddur A Jewish prayer book.

Simcha A joyous occasion; a celebration, usually related to a lifecycle event.

Simchat Bat Literally, "celebration of a daughter" in Hebrew. A celebration of the birth of a Jewish baby girl.

Smicha/Semikah A rabbinical ordination.

Sukkah Literally "booth" or "hut" in Hebrew. The temporary dwelling in which Jews live during the holiday of Sukkot.

Sukkot Literally "booths" or "huts" in Hebrew. The fall holiday commemorating the forty years spent by the Jews wandering in the desert before entering the land of Israel. The main ritual of Sukkot is the construction of huts similar to those in which the Jews lived in the desert and "dwelling" (which usually means eating and sleeping, weather permitting) in them for a week.

Tallit A Jewish prayer shawl worn by men during service in the synagogue.

Tanakh The entire Jewish bible including the Torah, Prophets, and Writings (Tanakh is an acronym of the names of the three sections of the bible: Torah, Nevi'im and Kethuvim).

Tefillin Small black boxes containing sections of the shema attached to leather straps and worn around the head and arm during prayer. Also called "phylacteries."

Treif The opposite of "kosher," meaning impure, as in not adhering to Jewish dietary laws.

Tzadik/Tzadika A righteous man/woman.

Yeshiva A seminary for Jewish studies.

Yom Kippur The Day of Atonement, the most important day in the Jewish calendar.

INTRODUCTION

A few months after I had entered high school, the boys with the boots showed up. I called them that because they had paired their historically accurate Hitler Jugend uniforms with shiny 10-hole Dr. Martens, white laces dramatically contrasting their perfect oxblood shade.

I could always hear them approaching, the boys with the boots. The sound of rubber soles against linoleum would cut through the noises of my high school hallway, and as soon as I turned around, there they were.

My family had settled in that sleepy Swedish coastal town some seventy years earlier, leaving the big city for a better place to raise a family. The war came, and what happened after that I only know through scattered pictures and hushed-down questions. I was told life had become difficult, so they adapted, as the children of their children would also be taught to do.

The boys with the boots would talk to me sometimes. Without a hint of aggression they would tell me that my relatives had become soap in camps, not too far away from where we stood, and that I should follow suit. There was no physical violence, not even once. Instead they would sit next to me in the cafeteria, wait for me at the top of the stairs, or stand to attention as I passed by them. I didn't know why they despised me, but I knew that it mattered. It mattered to them, and so, it had to matter to me.

When I was fifteen years old, I shaved my head. It was a last resort, a final measure, after spending years changing for and adapting to a world that seemed set on viewing me as a stranger. I had tried so hard. Taming the wild, dark curls, bleaching and straightening to resemble the shiny blonde girls. It didn't help; neither did hiding in bathrooms and libraries to escape the silent warfare that recess had come to be. It was as if the more I altered myself to be like them, the more they despised me for even trying.

The whole process took over two hours, and when I finally met my own gaze in the bathroom mirror I could see that the venture had been in vain. All the traits I had grown to despise—the big nose, the wide mouth, and the bushy black eyebrows—were all the more visible without the aid of untamed hair. That was the night I realized there was nothing I could do to change what made me deserve all this hatred. It was also the first and last time I ever saw my mother cry.

My mother sat me down and told me that once, when she was just a little girl, she had gone driving with her father. Suddenly she had asked him what it meant that they were Jewish, and why all the children at school were telling her that she was. Her father had slapped her across the face and yelled, "Don't ever say that word again! If anyone asks, we are Walloons. That's what you tell them. Walloons." They rode back to the house in silence, and my mother did not broach the subject again.

The history of my family has shaped me and, ironic as it may seem, the hatred that I was subjected to during my adolescence actually helped form my Jewish identity and confront me with who and what I am: a Jew in the diaspora, a survivor among survivors, and a link in a vast chain that spans across the world. The hatred I faced—that all Jews face—made me start asking the questions that led me to the writing of this book: what make us special; what makes us stay Jewish despite all of this; and why have we survived through the ages when every age has offered up another threat to our existence.

In the past few years, Europe has exploded, from gruesome murders in Belgium and France to riots, torched synagogues and defaced

Holocaust memorial sites, along with a dramatic spike in hate crimes all over the continent. Jews are being singled out and persecuted, once again. Most recently, Paris and Copenhagen were added to the list of cities synonymous with terror, as more Jewish blood was spilled before the eyes of the world. In response to these escalating threats, many have called for a universal Aliyah, a return to Israel, saying that we Jews have no home in the diaspora. But the truth is that it has been our home since the Babylonian Exile, and that we diaspora Jewry carry many different identities within us.

The boys with the boots were on a mission to scare me, to make me feel shame over my Jewishness and to hide in the shadows like so many other Jews before me. For whatever reason, they accomplished the opposite and set me on a mission of my own: to solve the puzzle of my own identity as an exile and a citizen, a Jew and a Swede, and to turn the darkness I was taught into a light among our scattered nation.

For too long, the Jewish diaspora has been described as a problem to be solved, but with this book, I wanted to show the other side of our beautiful Jewish people and highlight the history, culture, and lives of my brothers and sisters all across the world. This is more than a book for me, more than a cultural project; this is my reply to the boys with the boots—the pushback I was too scared and vulnerable to offer at the time.

The communities represented here are of course not a full representation of the diaspora; communities of great historical importance such as Iraq were unavailable to me due to security concerns, and others had to be neglected due to time constraints. What I have tried to do with this project is offer as comprehensible an image as possible, showing a wide array of social, economic, and geographical circumstances. Any areas or countries not covered in this book should not be seen as a reflection of their importance to me or the Jewish people.

Today, I wear my big, curly hair with pride, and I embrace all the facets of my being. I feel gratitude toward the boys in the boots for confronting me with this identity and, in essence, bringing me closer to my people. Were it not for those boys, I may have been another statistic, another European Jew faded into the woodwork. Instead, I am a proud representative of my brothers and sisters, and this book is my love letter to them.

DJERBA

Adir is guiding me through the labyrinth that is Hara Kbira town, annoyed, because we're late for the Hanukkah candle lighting, right after Shabbat. The man hosting us is a leader within the community, described by those who know him as a modest *macher*. When we finally get there, half of the island's Jews seem to be cramped inside his humble, white stone house.

Before I lose track, I count eleven cats in the house, all in various stages of age and care. The house is chaotic, yet warm, and a TV is on in the combined bedroom and living room, blaring what seems to be the Tunisian version of *The Voice*. There are Israeli and Tunisian flags on almost every surface and framed pictures of rabbis I don't recognize on every wall.

Our host is dressed in traditional Tunisian garb, a full-length *djellabah* and a matching fez, and you can tell his standing in the community by the way everyone orbits around him, hanging on every word of his elaborate blessings. Adir, usually full of a young man's swagger, is quiet and submissive in this setting. He falls back for his elder, and, without really knowing why, I follow suit.

Everyone says the blessing in unison, and while we're singing, the minarets start wailing, calling all Muslims to prayer. I'm the only one to react, losing my momentum a bit; the others go on as if the loud Arabic is nothing more than white noise. Once we're done, I make a comment to Adir about the interruption, saying the call to prayer threw me off. He doesn't really answer; instead he points out that the front door has been open this whole time.

"There is nothing to fear from the outside for the Jews of Tunisia. Could you say the same about Europe?"

Point taken.

Placed atop the African continent, just a couple of hours flight from the major European capitals and a stone's throw from the Middle East, Tunisia has historically been vulnerable to invasion and cultural influence from all sides. It seems as if anyone with ambitions of greatness has, at some point, passed through Tunisia: from the Vandals, to the Byzantines and Phoenicians, Romans, Jews, Arabs, Spaniards and Turks to, most recently, the French. Even though the Muslim Arabs clearly won the war for Tunisia's identity—ninety-eight percent of the population is Sunni Muslim—everyone who passed through, conquered, or colonized left a cultural indentation on the country's soul, making it a sparkly kaleidoscope of human history.

Tunisia is both the smallest and the richest of the African countries, despite its meager natural resources, and it has amassed its riches through agriculture and by using its geographical advantage—being reachable from Europe, the Middle East, and the rest of the African continent—to build its modern economy on trade and tourism.

I arrive in Djerba, a beautiful Mediterranean island just off the coast of mainland Tunisia, on the first day of Hanukkah. The island is truly a hidden gem, its picture-perfect beaches and picturesque villages relatively undiscovered by Western tourists, and traveling there feels almost like traveling through time.

Though I packed my own candles and hanukkiah, it turns out that I will never use them once. That first night, I venture out of my hotel to take in the city lights. Just a few steps into the walkabout, my eyes fall on a shop called "Shimon Bijouterie," and I'm immediately drawn inside. Met by an explosion of color, from the painted ceiling to the heavy gold necklaces hanging from the thick, stone-clad walls,

I'm struck by two men standing at the counter—one older, with thick, silver hair; one younger, with hair as dark as night. The older man is dominant and charming, schmoozing the customers and running the show, while the younger stands always a step or two behind him, shy but intense in that low-key mysterious way. They are quite obviously family—the resemblances are clear as day—and while I wait my turn, I watch the relatable scene of a son and a father, the submissive and the dominant, working together in a harmony that must have taken half a lifetime to perfect.

My French is rusty, but we get by. Alternating between French and Hebrew, I learn that this is one of several Jewish jewelry shops in the neighborhood of Houmt Souk, and that Shimon and his son Avi Chay are the third generation of Djerba Jews to manage this particular establishment.

Shimon sees my Magen David necklace and smiles. Given my broken Hebrew, he asks if I'm Jewish—and how in the world did I end up here?

I tell him my story, and, without skipping a beat, he exclaims, "OK, then. Let's go light some candles together."

Avi Chay closes the shop doors, and we stroll out almost immediately. It's not an oddity here to lock up shop several times a day to accommodate for the varied and disparate religious practices of this unique place. Djerba, small as it is, contains Muslims, Jews and Christians, and while radically different, all three groups are living a traditional and observant life. Everyone here is religious in some way, and all the shopkeepers have a prayer schedule to which they adhere. We walk together through the narrow streets of the market, and there—just around the corner—is a bright blue door leading to one of the most beautiful synagogues I have ever seen.

It's tiny, really, just two small rooms with a large *bima* in the middle, all of it slathered in white and blue tiles. To my left is a metallic hanukkiah, and next to it a large Coca Cola bottle filled with oil. As the men begin to file in, I withdraw to the back, watching them put on their *tallitot* and prepare.

Then they start singing, and I'm taken aback by how the Jewish prayers are sung with Arabic-style melodies. These are not the traditional Ashkenazi songs that I am used to, moving from word to word in an orderly fashion. Instead, there is evocative wailing, the clear telling of a story where every word is saturated with meaning and experienced anew, each time. It is exotic and wonderful and somewhat meditative in nature. It's both louder and more joyous than I'm used to. Despite being the only woman in this *shul* in a strange and faraway land, I can't help but join in.

Our Journey to Djerba

Legend says that when Emperor Nebuchadnezzar II destroyed Solomon's Temple in Jerusalem in 586 BCE, members of the Jewish priestly class, the Kohanim, settled on the island of Djerba in present-day Tunisia. The Kohanim carried with them a vestige of the destroyed Temple and placed it in the synagogue they built on the island. The El Ghriba synagogue, as it is called, became a place not just of worship, but of pilgrimage. In fact, the yearly pilgrimage to the island of the Kohanim is a tradition that still takes place today among religious Jews from around the world.

Djerba is an isolated place, and, given its prominence in Jewish history, it can be said to host one of the most genuine and traditional expressions of Jewish life in the world. Djerba is also unique in that it is one of the few places in the region still considered home to a contingent of Arab Jews.

Prior to 1948, the Middle East and Africa were home to approximately 850,000 Jews, but today, the Arab world's Jewish population has dwindled to a mere 4,500; and it is still falling. Countries that historically housed the largest Jewish populations—like Egypt, Iraq, Algeria, and Libya—have virtually no Jews living within their borders anymore. Morocco was once home to 265,000 Jewish citizens. By 2017, only 2,500 Jews remained, many of whom were above fifty years of age. While Djerba's Jewish population may not be the very last of the Arab world's Jews, it is certainly a last beacon of hope in a part of the world where Jews have been driven out, killed, or forcibly assimilated and converted *en masse.*

I walk back from shul with Shimon and Avi Chay, and on our way we pass a large group of Muslim men coming back from prayer. I ask Shimon if it's difficult here—being openly Jewish—and he shrugs and tells me that it's easier here than most places with a Muslim majority.

"People know that we are Jews, and they leave us alone for the most part. We have found an equilibrium that works."

That equilibrium consists of a "separate but equal" system, where the Jews live together in the town of Hara Kbira and work in the nearby town of Houmt Souk. They keep to themselves, but there seems to be very little animosity from the Arab majority, at least on the outside.

"There are things we just don't discuss, like Israel, for example," explains Shimon. "Even when we talk about it amongst ourselves, we don't say 'Israel'; we say 'the land,' and we never engage in political conversations with our non-Jewish neighbors."

It's not unlike the way Jews interact in many other places around the world, including in my own country. We say "Eretz" when discussing Israel and "cousins" rather than "Arabs" so as not to alert anyone within earshot to the fact that we are Jewish. Diaspora Jews have always used a sort of code-language to stay safe, and the Jews of Djerba are no exception.

The next day I meet up with Avi Chay again. He has promised to show me the kosher restaurant in Houmt Souk, and once we arrive, I am surprised by how familiar it feels.

In the small one-room restaurant, three older men sit at a table, loudly debating some important affair of state while sipping hot black coffee that spills over the rim of their glass cups. This could be a scene from Jerusalem, where the "parliaments" gather at cafés—semi-permanent groups of coffee comrades who ponder and debate family and national politics alike over double espressos on Friday mornings. The difference between this scene and one in Jerusalem is that the men here are all dressed in traditional and somewhat outdated clothes: traditional hats, Tunisian leather slippers, tunic-style shirts. Outside, the restaurant staff is cooking meat on a makeshift grill placed directly on the pavement. The cook is wearing a black *kippah*, and he smiles as he brings me dish after delicious dish. He stands to the side as I eat, watching my joy with undisguised excitement. I am transported to another world as I bite into the traditional Tunisian *brik*—a delicacy of deep-fried phyllo dough stuffed with eggs, spices, herbs, and tuna. The egg breaks as I bite into the dough, the yolk runs down my hand and sticks to the crevices of my rings, and I desperately try to keep some shred of dignity as I enjoy the food's rich texture and flavors. The next dish is a Tunisian take on the Moroccan *Chraime*—a traditional Sephardi dish with whitefish and hot peppers. About a minute into dunking the crusty bread into hot tomato sauce, I realize that the Tunisian take is far spicier than any of the Moroccan versions I have previously eaten. My eyes tear up and start running uncontrollably, and neither the staff nor the guests hide their amusement as I desperately wipe down my face and dab my tongue with bread to stop the burning.

While finishing my meal, I look up to see a young man enter the café. I am immediately struck by his Western-style appearance—jeans, a Polo shirt and stylish glasses give the impression that he's just walked out of an American yeshiva. He greets me in perfect English—an oddity in these parts—and asks if he can join my table.

His name is Adir, and he turns out to be Avi Chay's cousin, recently returned from four years at a yeshiva in London. He now lives in Bara Kbira with his family—mother, father, two brothers, and four sisters—and runs one of the Jewish jewelry shops in the nearby village. I ask Adir why he thinks Djerba is one of the few Arab lands where the Jewish community is actually growing and seemingly thriving. Adir soberly explains that the Jews of Djerba understand the rules and limitations to which they must adhere. Their insularity, imposed and self-imposed in different measures, keeps them safe.

"It comes down to the rabbis, really," he begins.

"They set the limits for how much we can interact with the non-Jews; how observant we are of Jewish law. They help us stay strong and vigilant against the threats of assimilation."

It's not until I actually visit Hara Kbira, the almost exclusively Jewish town in Djerba, that I fully understand what he means by this. The Jews of Djerba have chosen isolation that millions of Jews across the world have been forced into and fought their way out of. They have chosen this ghetto-like village in order to protect their observance and their traditions; from the look of things, their strategy is working.

There are children in *kippot* playing soccer in the desolate streets. It's difficult to even explain how strange and moving it is to see that here, in Tunisia, but I stop to watch, enchanted by their carefree play. I couldn't see a scene like this one in Europe, and definitely not in my own country of Sweden. There, Jewish children dare not run around this identifiably *Jewish*, but here of all places, they do.

I ask Avi Chay which houses are Jewish; he laughs and says it's easier to show me which ones aren't. He points to three houses, sprinkled across the Jewish neighborhood where the entirety of Djerba's Jewish population lives.

We walk from synagogue to synagogue. There are twelve of them in this one small village. Each of the buildings appear humble from the outside in contrast to their gloriously colorful interiors, a stark difference from Ashkenazi synagogues, which often have grand exteriors and functional internal layouts. While this discretion partly relates to the fact that the synagogues in Muslim-majority countries have had to operate covertly, it is also one of many illustrations of how the vibrant nature of Sephardi and Mizrahi cultural and religious expression diverge from Germanic simplicity.

The synagogues of Hara Kbira lack the airs of the La Ghriba synagogue, situated on the outskirts of the main town, but they make up for it in *yiddishkeit* and life. La Ghriba is Djerba's most famous Jewish structure, and a beautiful one at that, but it is no longer an active place of prayer, instead serving as a museum—a relic of what once was, following an Al Qaida terrorist attack in 2002. La Ghriba is heavily guarded, and I must pass through a military-style checkpoint to gain entry. This is the only synagogue on the island where even unmarried women are expected to cover their hair, and a Muslim gate-keeper hands me a shawl as I walk in.

A sea of blue and green washes the walls and dark wooden benches sitting beneath mosaic arches. Heavy chandeliers light up the room. I have perhaps never been further from a European aesthetic and never fallen more immediately in love with a synagogue. It is too much, but, at the same time, just perfect. The three main rooms are linked by a stone walkway and there, in the third and final alcove, the morning sun floods through the stained-glass windows and hits what looks like hundreds of pieces of shining silver.

And yet, for all the wonder, there is an unnerving sense that this place has been made a theatre for tourists. Even the three men sitting and praying feel like props for effect. La Ghriba no longer has a *minyan*—the ten men necessary for Jewish prayer—but the synagogue is packed when the tourists arrive for Lag Ba'omer to participate in elaborate pilgrimage-like festivities organized by the Jewish community and the tourism board of Tunisia. Even then, it serves only as a house of interfaith prayer.

I pay a small fee to be allowed to walk in and look at the *aron kodesh*, the walled cabinet that holds not only the Torah scrolls but also the artifact claimed to come from the Holy Temple. Even closed, it is a sight to behold.

On the *bima* sit flowing silken scarves in brilliant colors, interspersed with whimsically arranged bouquets of flowers.

The ancient story of the fleeing Kohanim notwithstanding, ample evidence documents Jewish life in Tunisia as early as 200 CE, and archeological findings prove the existence of a Jewish community in Carthage under Roman rule. The sages of the Talmud also reference this place as their home from the second to fourth centuries, another reason we know of the significant Jewish presence in Tunisia at that time.

The strength of the Jewish community in ancient Tunisia is also reflected in the measures Roman rulers implemented to afflict it. As the Jewish presence grew following the destruction of the Second Temple, the Romans divided the Jews into clans and taxed them according to profession. Special laws restricted their Jewish life and movement—a story that repeats itself, time after time, ruler after ruler, until the Spanish Inquisition.

By the end of the sixteenth century, many Jews had already deserted the coastal areas of Tunisia and Morocco and fled to the Berber communities in the mountains and desert, hoping to find a more peaceful home. But even then, the Djerban Jews were the exception to the rule, staying put by the sea. Rather than dispersing in the mountains, they huddled in place, and their strategy seems to be the same now as it was back then. One could imagine that it would, at least at some point, have been tempting to spread out among the locals on the island, hiding in plain sight. Instead, the Jews here chose to settle in the town of Hara Kbira, as a pack rather than lone wolves.

The synagogues in Hara Kbira are perhaps not as adorned as La Ghriba or even as beautiful, but they are bubbling with the chaos of daily religious life. The first one I walk into has a yeshiva in the adjoining room, and inside a man sits, deep in learning over a Talmudic tractate. In the next, someone is stacking green plastic chairs after services, offering us tea and chatting with my guide in fast-paced Arabic. The third synagogue is empty, so I sit there for a while, just taking it all in. An antique menorah sits to one side, next to a door leading to a permanent sukkah. There are books everywhere—tattered copies rather than the impeccable collections I saw at La Ghriba—and someone left their sweater to dry on top of an old water-filled radiator. A calendar lists weekly community events, many of the sort one might find at any other synagogue in nearly any other part of the Jewish world. There are Torah studies on Sunday morning; an all-female challah-bake meets on Thursday night.

Avi Chay now shows me the local kosher eateries and proudly points out that all the local food vendors have at least a few items that are on their Tunisian kosher list. Coming from Sweden, this seems to be almost an upside-down world, where the majority of Muslims in the town cater to the needs of their local Jews.

But perhaps that's also something of an exaggeration here. A large military presence is posted at the entrances to the Jewish village. The

Tunisian government has made the safety of the Jewish population a priority, but that sentiment isn't necessarily mirrored in the views of the common man.

I ask my new friend what he thinks of the security measures, and surprisingly he tells me he wishes they weren't there, in a comment echoing a sentiment heard through centuries of Jewish persecution.

"I hate that it draws so much attention to us," he explains. "It makes it look as if we have something to hide, or something we don't want anyone else to have, and I think maybe it causes more problems than it solves."

This is a common problem for the Jews in the diaspora; wanting to be integrated, but not assimilated. The necessary protection measures themselves perpetuate this sense of separateness, causing the community to fall further into isolation. What I saw in Hara Kbira was a Tunisian version of an old-school European *shtetl*, built by choice and not only necessity; a world within a world and relative stability in a volatile region.

Persecution and Assimilation for Tunisian Jews

Isolation or assimilation is just one in a long line of difficult choices that the Jews of Tunisia have faced since the seventh and eighth century when Islam became the established law of the land. As in the entire Muslim world, Jews and Christians were either forced to convert to Islam or live as *dhimmis*—second-class citizens. Depending on the country, they would be allowed to practice their religion and keep their customs, but they would remain submissive to Muslim rule and pay a *dhimmi*-tax to save their lives and spare their property and livelihoods from destruction.

After centuries of suffering under brutal caliphates, things went from bad to worse for the Jews of Tunis with the advent of the Almohad Caliphate. During this period, mass conversions and massacres became commonplace and, at the instruction of the Jewish sage Maimonides, Tunisian Jews were told to hide their religious affiliation and practice in secret while outwardly professing allegiance to Islam. Though many heeded Maimonides' call, there was also widespread Islamization of the Jewish community under the Almohad Caliphate, and an endless amount of Jewish lives were lost in the process through killings, conversions, and assimilation.

The first signs of real improvement came only during the modern era with the reign of Ahmed Bey, which began in 1837. He and his successor, Mohammed Bey, implemented liberal legislation that did away with the punitive measures that had been imposed on the Jews. Under both Ahmed and Mohammed Bey, a large number of Jews rose to positions of political power within Tunisian society and government as poets, politicians, ambassadors and masters of trade. Most importantly, Mohammed Bey issued a constitution according to which all Tunisians, regardless of race or creed, were granted equal rights.

Tunisia came under French protectorate in 1881 and its Jews were, for all intents and purposes, emancipated. Unfortunately, it was one step forward and two steps back for the Jews of Tunisia. By the 1940s, the country came under Vichy rule and the Jews were yet again subject to anti-Semitic laws, which dictated where and if the Jews could live, work, and worship.

German forces occupied Tunisia in November 1942 and immediately arrested Moises Burgel, the president of the Tunis Jewish community, along with several other prominent Jews. While many Jews were deported to Nazi camps and had their property seized by the government between November 1942 and May 1943, the Jews of Vichy Tunisia were comparatively spared the mass deportation their European counterparts suffered.

Though the Jews of Tunisia did not escape the Holocaust unscathed, they endured only to reap more hardship in the years to follow. While Tunisia gained independence in 1956, there was little independence to be had for the country's Jewish population. In 1957, the government destroyed the Jewish quarter of Tunis, and the rabbinical tribunal and Jewish community councils were abolished. A few years later, as retaliation during the Six-Day War in Israel, Muslims torched the Great

Synagogue of Tunis to the ground. Since 1957, there has been a steady stream of Jewish immigration from Tunisia to France and Israel—except for the Jews of Djerba.

Staying Put Despite Adversity

The resilient residents of the island of the Kohanim have seen their share of troubles, the most famous of which was the La Ghriba synagogue attack. On April 11, 2002, a truck full of explosives was detonated close to the ancient synagogue, killing nineteen people and wounding another thirty.

Other than the deadly La Ghriba attack, Tunisia enjoyed calm and growth in the first years of the twenty-first century, but a decade in, that calm would turn to chaos. In 2011, Tunisia became the first country to start what would be known as the Arab Spring, a series of popular protests and uprisings against dictatorships. Tunisia's Jasmine Revolution marked the end of the repressive and corrupt rule of President Zine El Abidine Ben Ali. Ben Ali, a neo-liberal, had been the first elected president after Tunisia gained independence, and his autocratic style had, for all its faults, helped keep Tunisia's disparate Islamist parties and interests in check. After the Jasmine Revolution, the rift between secular and religious interests seemed to be throwing the country into another bout of chaos, but moderate Islamists played a crucial role in stabilizing it by calming both sides and forming an interim coalition.

In a bid to show off its new and progressive ways, the interim Tunisian government and its ruling Muslim democratic Ennahda Party sent a representative to the Jews in Djerba, assuring them they would be able to live safely under the democratic Islamist rule of the new leadership.

Despite this commendable effort, anti-Semitic incidents and attacks spiked in the year following the Jasmine Revolution. Tensions grew so extreme that the Israeli Knesset announced it had allocated funding to help Tunisian Jews relocate to Israel.

A few years later, in 2014, the Ennahda party stepped down, having failed to implement its platform of Islamism paired with multi-party democracy. Pending democratic elections, a new secular constitution was drafted that not only included provisions for freedom of religion and conscience but also explicitly protected religious minorities from all forms of harassment and discrimination. It has been hailed as a model for other Arab countries. In 2015, the Tunisian National Dialogue Quartet, a four-party alliance created to govern post-revolution Tunisia, was awarded the Nobel Peace Prize for "its decisive contribution to the building of a pluralistic democracy in Tunisia in the wake of the Tunisian Revolution of 2011."

Today

Modern-day Jewish life in Tunisia is in part made possible by its geographic isolation. Just as the geographical distance from Nazi camps offered some form of safety during World War II, Tunisian Jewry is somewhat removed from the plagues of the twenty-first century. In Djerba, the Jews are able to keep to strict rules governing their religious lifestyle and culture. Options to leave are scarce for the many who lack education and funds, and the inhabitants of Djerba tend to remain on the island, some never leaving even for a short vacation. There are of course exceptions, like Adir, where families invest in their sons to gain a better and more extensive education abroad than they ever could in Tunisia, but the sons return to serve the community they left. As Adir and the others explained to me, returning is a willing choice as much as it is an obligation. They return because they believe that Djerba can offer them something that the outside world cannot.

There is no divorce here, no assimilation, and no wayward children being left unattended by parents too busy to show up. For better or worse, no one is ever alone, and the center of everything is the Jewish family and the traditions they live to uphold. As an island, Djerba offers the environment required to maintain a cohesive, unassimilated Jewish community.

Jewish women in Djerba have an average of four children each, and some have as many as ten. As a result, the Jewish population has grown significantly in the past decade, and fifty percent of the community is aged twenty or younger. A comparison between Djerba and Tunis reveals how much of an outlier the island of the Kohanim really is, as the latter has gone from ten thousand to four hundred Jews, most of them fifty years old or older.

This new lease on Jewish life is reflected in the Sayada house, proudly placed in the center of Tunisia's own Jerusalem, Hara Kbira. I've been invited to Adir's house in Hara Kbira for Shabbat, and to spend the weekend sharing a room with his four sisters at his parents' home around the corner. When I first walk in, I feel slightly awkward and out of place. The house is bustling with activity. Just hours before Shabbat, the women and girls are busy preparing the last of the food for the weekend. I look around the house and see small fish statues everywhere, from simple clay sculptures to a gigantic silver fish adorning the dining room sideboard. In this seaside community, the fish—like the *hamsa*, or "hand of God"—is said to protect you from the evil eye and bring good fortune. Traditionally, when fish were plentiful, it was said that this was a display of the good will of God.

The home is warm, but socially there is ice to be broken. Suddenly, the oldest sister asks me if she can do my makeup, and quickly, chattering young women between the ages of twelve and eighteen surround me. They apply blush, lipstick, and intensely black kohl eyeliner to my eyes. I look in the mirror, and I hardly recognize myself: I have beautiful Arabic-style eye makeup and my hair is up in a large bun, courtesy of the Sayada sisters.

"Oooh, *tu es si belle!*" they squeal, and I feel part of the family. Avia, the oldest sister, shows me a picture of her with a young man and tells me that she just got engaged. Avia is seventeen years old, about par for the course in a community where most women get engaged in their late teens and the men in their early twenties. Avia and her sisters are beautiful and, to a Swede, they seem amazingly happy and content. Their home and this village are their universe, and for a moment, I envy the closeness and simplicity of their lives.

I ask Adir to take me to the synagogue for Friday night services, apparently an unusual request. Women don't usually go to synagogue in Djerba unless it's the High Holidays. Women attending a regular Shabbat service are considered peculiar and progressive. He takes me, though, and arranges for me to sit in an adjacent room so I can hear the prayers while keeping to local tradition. The synagogue doesn't have a *mechitze*, a barrier meant to separate men's and women's seating. Adir asks me to walk a minute or two ahead of him on the way to synagogue, as it is unacceptable for two single people of the opposite sex to walk together alone in the streets of the Jewish neighborhood.

The prayer service here is radically different than anything I've ever encountered—not only the melodies, but the order as well. A man walks into the room and, breaking protocol, he helps me find the right passage. We share a smile that transcends language and culture.

This simple gesture sums up my entire experience in Djerba: its people displaying warmth and kindness and genuine curiosity at the difference I represent while staunchly maintaining their particular brand of Orthodoxy.

The prayers wind to a close, and we return to the house to find the Sayada sisters standing at the doorway dressed to the nines—high heels and brightly colored dresses accessorized with heavy silver jewelry. They ask me to go with them to *dorra-dorra*. I follow along, feeling interested, confused, and severely underdressed for whatever the occasion may be.

Turns out, *dorra-dorra* is a walk of meaning and ceremony. On Shabbat, between every meal, everyone in the Jewish community walks up and down the one major street in Hara Kbira to see and be seen. The whole walk takes about four minutes at a slow pace. Once you reach the end, you turn around and do it all over again.

The sisters introduce me to the entire community as their cousin. I immediately realize the extent of the closeness on this island. They live with each other, marry each other and, at least if you're a girl, you don't leave the country—and definitely not on your own—the sisters tell me as much while we're walking. There are other signs of their isolation here; I see several people with birth deformities just on this street, and though I cannot claim to have a statistically sound sample, it seems to be well above average.

"That's my fiancé," Avia discretely nods toward a young man I recognize from the pictures in her bedroom. They're about to be married, but instead of greeting him, we just walk on by. I ask her why they don't walk together or even say hello. And again, the strict self-discipline of the Jewish community is manifest in her answer.

"Boys and girls don't interact; we meet with friends or family a few times when we are courting, but between the engagement and the wedding we are not allowed to meet, and we don't even acknowledge each other and say hello."

Carefully as I can, I ask why they would do it this way and how it can be kept up. Avia and her sisters tell me that these are the necessary boundaries to keep their traditions alive.

"If you let boys and girls meet after the engagement, things will get out of hand and they will relax, and soon, the bride is pregnant at the wedding!"

It may seem extreme to someone from a more modern setting, but the logic ultimately makes sense. The fifteen hundred Jews on this island need to protect themselves from assimilation; they are literally fighting for their lives, and the rules and limitations they adhere to are all part of that fight. This level of conservativism keeps the Jewish girls and boys of Djerba in line—because once they lose their grip, they may end up losing everything.

We walk back and forth on this one street for almost two hours, and I contemplate the larger meaning of what I see and hear. These communities may be small, but they hold the distilled version of what we are as a people; they take responsibility for our entire tribe, keeping our traditions pure—sometimes at a great personal cost.

There is also a disturbing hint of Arab honor culture in this that I cannot stay blind to or deny. For instance, the women and girls do not receive an education beyond their mid-teens, and their given role is to have many children and keep the home. It looks as if there is little choice involved. Then again, some of the girls do tell me that if they could date and travel, they would choose not to do it. One of Avia's friends explains that the modern life that other Jews enjoy seems to ruin their lives and their communities.

"We see that the Jews who move to Tunis just disappear," she tells me. "Once they leave Djerba, it's over. They're exposed to modern life and temptations, and soon they intermarry and go off the *derech* (path)."

We continue our walk, back and forth, and I'm somewhat amused by the fact that the men are so obviously watching us, and the women are so aware of being watched; but neither side will acknowledge the other. On this religious catwalk, many of the biggest decisions of family life are made. We call it a walk to guard against the obvious.

During the Shabbat dinner, I ask my hosts if there aren't any Jews in Djerba who choose to live a secular life or who fall off the path entirely. Shimon tells me no, at first. He then adds that yes, there a few, but they are no longer part of the community.

"Some Jews have moved to Houmt Souk and decided to not be Jews anymore, and we have a cemetery where we bury those who get divorced or other things of that nature."

This takes me aback a little, given that I myself am a divorced Jew who, in many ways, falls short in the eyes of the religiously perfect and divine. Life here is harsher, and that is the price of the closeness and warmth. You are all in, or all out, and to a Western Jew that is a very foreign concept.

Shimon goes on to say that divorce is very rare. If a couple considers divorce or a girl thinks about wanting to date like a Westerner, the entire community comes together to speak to them to ensure they make the right choice. With this coercive tough love as an accepted norm, I can't even imagine how difficult it must be to come into adulthood here with all the wants and needs that adolescence holds. Then again, perhaps the young Jews of Djerba do not even consider many of the issues that occupy my mind. They don't have to worry about finding a suitable partner, as this will be arranged for them. My own Western constant obsession with self-fulfillment and success doesn't really apply here, as a life on this island means defining success and happiness in entirely different ways—through ensuring the continuity of traditional Jewish families and community.

After dinner, I go back to the Sayada house, and the men go upstairs while we, the women, stay up and chat until the early hours of the morning. The thing about separating the sexes as much as they do here is that the closeness between women is extraordinary. I tell the Sayada women about my life, my divorce, my hopes and dreams, and they reciprocate. We are unbothered by the male world, and it's freeing and safe in a way I didn't anticipate. I ask the young sisters about the thoughts I've had on freedom and choice and the issues that other young Jews struggle with, but all I can get out of them is that they are happy. Maybe they're holding back because I'm a stranger, or perhaps that is all there is. Either way, I leave it be.

For the first time in forever I sleep until ten, and the sisters and I lounge around in our pajamas while saying our morning prayers. We set up for lunch and get changed, and when the men return from synagogue, I feel so much a part of the family that it's as if I've been waiting for them to come home too.

The Shabbat lunch is lively to say the least, and the food is probably the best I have ever had: liver-stuffed chicken fillets, spicy kebabs, and perfect, Persian-style rice. New dishes are heaped onto the table and we all go for seconds and thirds, to the enthusiastic praise of Adir's mother.

Even with this spread, I can hardly focus on anything but the beauty of the songs sung by Adir and his older brother. "This is what it's all about," I think to myself as I hear the Arabic intertwined with the Hebrew, literally and figuratively. *This* is why the Jews in these faraway places are worth protecting—the culture they hold and express is unique and ancient. The mix of Jewish and Arab culture, developed over millennia, expressed through everything from food to prayer and profession, almost entirely without modern, Western influence. I had heard so much about Jews in Arab lands before coming here, but always from the perspective of loss and humiliation. This community, however, is far from humiliated. Rather, it remains a proud vestige of Jewish continuity in a part of the world where this has long been deemed impossible.

Once Shabbat is over, I miss it. Usually, once the sun is about to set, I am ready for the new week and dying to get my phone out, but here I am comfortable in the bubble.

As a European Jew, I am used to feeling like an outsider. And yes, the Jews in Djerba are outsiders as well, but the main difference is that here they have created an impenetrable core that provides great comfort and relative safety. As I leave the Sayada house after Havdalah, I think to myself that this might be the future of the Jewish diaspora: to refuse modernity, hide from the outside world, and plant your feet firmly in the past.

UZBEKISTAN

About ten minutes into my walk, I realize that I'm lost.

I left my hotel thirty minutes before services are set to begin at the Bukharian synagogue, and even though Google Maps told me it was barely a twenty-minute walk, I am starting to panic as the quiet residential streets are exchanged for near-highway mayhem.

It's my first day in Tashkent and, through a friendly translator at the hotel, I have already announced to the local community that I'd be arriving at morning prayer service. I'm already running late, however, and the thought of leaving a bad first impression puts my *Jekker*-anxiety on immediate high alert.

So I grab a taxi, and I'm in a terrible mood that is only exacerbated by the fact that my cabbie Mahmoud doesn't understand where I'm going nor does he even recognize the name of the street. So I'm sitting there already annoyed by what I assume will be an extraordinary overcharge and stressed about what will happen when my driver realizes that we're headed to a Jewish house of prayer.

After a silent ten-minute drive, we get there, and Mahmoud points to the building and makes a face of recognition. I quickly grab a handful of cash and ask him what I owe, but to my confusion he shakes his head and smiles at me.

With the use of his phone and Google Translate, Mahmoud shows me a message, saying "No money. Please just say a prayer for Mahmoud when you are in there."

I ask him again, shocked, what I owe, but he closes my hand holding the money and makes a gesture toward the sky.

I have no way of thanking Mahmoud properly or conveying how deeply humbled I am, but I think about it all through services. How divine that meeting felt, to be called on my prejudice and misconceptions that way—to be met with nothing but humanity and respect. Believer to believer.

I had brought my European mindset and experiences to Central Asia and in that one moment had been proven wrong—as I would be many times in the week that followed. Without knowing it, Mahmoud had been the key to what ended up being a host of unexpected discoveries in Uzbekistan.

Many places claim to be ancient civilizations, but Uzbekistan can actually back that claim, having proof of human habitation in the region since around the Old Stone Age, some seventy thousand years ago. Thanks to the Amu River, the region was extraordinarily fertile, and throughout the first millennium, it attracted tribes that worked the soil and traded their goods along what we know as the Silk Road, connecting East and West.

This was a place that people and tribes passed through: Arabs in the 8th century, Mongols under Genghis Khan in the 13th century, Dzungars in the 15th–17th centuries, Persians in the 18th century, and finally the Russians in the late 19th century. Each passer-through left a small part of its society behind through influence and individuals and helped shape the melting pot we now know Uzbekistan to be. The name itself—Uzbekistan—was adopted by Turkish and Mongol immigrants during the early-to-mid 14th century, as an homage to the greatly admired Muslim ruler Özbeg (Uzbek) Khan, who was Khan of the western part of the Mongol Empire during that time. Özbeg Khan ruled over Mongolia at the height of the empire and was known for not only commanding one of the largest armies in the world but as a convert to Islam, to be welcoming and accepting of other faiths—especially Catholicism.

Once they were officially Uzbeks, the many disparate people of the region sought leadership that would unite them, and they found it in Abu'l-Khayr Khan, the young descendant of Genghis Khan who had taken it upon himself to consolidate the Central Asian tribes into a people. Under Abu'l-Khayr's rule, Uzbekistan grew and prospered, but he failed in his mission to fully unify the Uzbeks, spending much of his life fighting off opposition. Abu'l-Khayr was killed during the Dzungar invasion of 1468, and it wasn't until the sixteenth century that his grandson, Muhammad Shaybani, finally fulfilled his dream and founded the Shaybanid dynasty, conquering Samarkand, Bukhara, and the Afghani cities of Herat and Balkh in the process.

Though the following centuries contained turmoil, conquests, and rivaling dynasties from Asia to Persia, Uzbekistan grew to be a cultural and religious center in the region. Mosques and seminaries housed poets, scholars, and politicians, and the amassed riches of the rulers were spent on buildings, bridges, and houses of prayer. The tribes had become a people, and the villages had turned to cities. Once the growing Russian Empire started to throw its weight around the region, former enemies bound together to try and fight her off.

But they failed.

In 1868, Bukhara was invaded, and despite a few well-fought rebellions, seven years later Russia completed its conquest of the Uzbek territories, making the region a part of the Russian province of Turkistan. Although Uzbekistan was under official Russian rule, the Muslim hegemony persisted until the 1917 Russian Revolution. Muslim leaders tried to use the chaos and conflict that the revolution had brought with it to Turkistan and formed a resistance against the conquerors, but by 1921, Communist politicians ruled the two former capitals of Bukhara and Tashkent. The fight was, for all intents and purposes, over.

The Bolsheviks started redrawing the maps, and by 1925, Uzbekistan was one of the Central Asian territories within the Union of Soviet Socialist Republics (USSR). Tashkent, now the new capital, became a jewel in the Soviet crown and was flooded with Soviet bureaucrats and administrators, most of whom were from outside the immediate region. The purges began, and during the 1930s, an unknown number of political dissidents, minorities, and intellectuals were jailed, killed, or disappeared.

When World War II started, the demography of Uzbekistan changed as it became home to several major industries that were originally located west of the Ural Mountains as German forces invaded the Soviet Union in 1941, bringing thousands of Russian nationals with them. During the war, there was also an influx of ethnic Koreans, Crimean Tatars, and Chechens. These groups were later deported by orders of Stalin, and were accused by the central communists of disloyalty or, as in the case with the Chechens of Caucasus, outright treason. 144,000 people died as a direct result of the deportations, and in 1991, the Russian Federation declared that the deportation of minorities during Joseph Stalin's reign was an act of genocide.

But there was another side of Uzbekistan during the War. While the Red Army was fighting Hitler, more than one million Jewish refugees from Nazi-occupied Eastern Europe passed through Uzbekistan. Uzbekistan claims to have taken in 430,000 Jews, many of whom were orphaned children; those children were taken in and raised by Uzbek families. This remains a point of pride for not only Uzbek authorities but also the citizens of Uzbekistan, and it is said to have heavily influenced the way Muslims relate to Jews in the country to this day.

World War II left a mark on everyone, regardless of his or her background. From 1941 to 1945, 1,433,230 Uzbeks fought in the Red Army against Nazi Germany, and 500,000 lives were lost, military as well as civilian. 500,000 of the soldiers were Jewish (167,000 of them in command positions) and two hundred thousand Jewish soldiers lost their lives fighting in the war. The Uzbeks—Muslim, Christian, and Jewish—fought as equals, and they died as equals.

In 1953, Joseph Stalin died and with him, some of the cruelty and absolutism he championed. After the death of the despot, Tashkent started opening up from its isolation, receiving non-communist visitors for the first time since becoming part of the USSR, but the country remained under the firm control of the Communist Party for almost forty more years.

Since declaring independence in 1991, Uzbekistan has struggled with the concept of democracy, accepting another strongman as its leader, this time in the form of President Islam Karimov. The formerly diverse country began to lose its minorities, including Jews, Crimean Tatars, Greeks, Meskhetian Turks, and Slavs, who saw the post-Soviet state become increasingly ethnocentric and racist. At the same time, Islamic militants tried to gain control of the country, leading to an outbreak of violence and persecution of dissenting Muslims. Karimov ruled Uzbekistan until his death in 2016, and during his tenure, the country drew international condemnation for state-run forced labor, strong-arm tactics against political dissidents, crackdowns on free speech, and suppression of political and human rights.

Uzbekistan's current President, Shavkat Mirziyoyev, won his post in an election that was deemed corrupt and illegitimate by foreign observers, and while he has done much to open the country to the West, much of the old country has influenced the new regime.

In its 2018 report, Freedom House listed Uzbekistan as one of the twelve countries to have the worst aggregate scores on their *World Freedom Index*, referring to it as a "hermetic police state." There is little to no freedom of press, political, or civil liberties, and through its relentless crackdowns on what the government calls "religious extremism," it has engaged in extrajudicial jailings, interrogations, and outright torture. Despite its ongoing fight against extremism, several violent Islamic groups have strongholds in Uzbekistan, most notably Hizb ut-Tahrir and ISIS.

* * *

When I head to the synagogue again, this time for Shabbat services, I'm only the third to arrive.

I am shown to the women's balcony by a somber elderly man that I will later get to know as the president of the Bukharian Jewish community, and while I sit there taking it all in more and more men gather below me.

The synagogue décor reminds me of what I've seen in Iran: gold pillars mixed with dark wood and red velvet trimmings, all lit by heavy, sparkling chandeliers. What's different from the Iranian synagogues I've visited is the freezing cold, and even though a massive fan is attempting to heat the space, most of us keep our jackets on for the duration of the almost four-hour-long service. I expect the praying to feel foreign, but it doesn't; I follow along and can even pick up the mix of Russian, Uzbek, and Hebrew that is spoken in between prayers. It's a familiar chatter, the kind you hear in every synagogue in any town—arguing about the order of service or yelling at someone for forgetting to stand during the mourner's prayer.

I stick out like a sore thumb up there on my balcony, and every man that walks in looks up, does a double-take, and then nods graciously in my direction. I'm the only woman there that day and, judging by their reactions, perhaps the only woman to grace those halls in quite some time. The man reading from the Torah glances up at me every once in a while, and suddenly he yells out to me, asking for my Hebrew name.

A little taken aback, I shout it back to him, and he gives me a blessing between the Torah-readings, a clear sign of welcoming and respect. I'm moved, and the man is clearly pleased—I have a vague feeling that I have just experienced a very subtle form of Uzbek Orthodox flirtation.

After services, I'm invited for Kiddush, and when I'm seated at the table in a small communal room next door to the synagogue, I sort of wish I could be live-casting the moment. There I am, dressed in my best Shabbat dress, surrounded by twenty-five Bukhari men in much more sensible and warm clothing, staring at me, as if I were an exotic bird. It's even colder in this room, and the door is slightly ajar, pushing icy breezes in my direction. When I dig my hands into my pockets, I thank God that I remembered to bring my Swedish winter gloves. One of the men at the table speaks English, and he starts translating the questions that come at me, about who I am, and why I'm there, and how many eggs would I like to begin with? Turns out, a lot of eggs is the only right answer, as boiled eggs, along with fried carp, seem to be the staple dish of a Bukharian Kiddush.

As everyone around me keeps piling food on my plate and pouring vodka into my drinking-bowl, I get the low-down on the conflict between the Ashkenazi and Bukharian Sephardi communities, and it reminds me of the usual Jewish in-fighting, with heightened levels of racial and political strife.

There is a sense that these Jews are fighting not only for their traditions but for their very survival, as only five hundred of them remain here in Uzbekistan, a nation of just over thirty-two million. Just forty years ago, forty thousand Bukharian Jews lived in Soviet Uzbekistan, but since the fall of the wall most of them have left for either America or Israel.

The Bukharians

Bukharian Jews have a long and proud history in the region. Depending on who you ask, Jews arrived in the region either around 500 BCE as part of the Babylonian exodus from Israel or 730 BCE with the lost Israelite tribes of Issachar and Naphtali who were exiled from the Land of Israel by the Assyrian kings Tiglath-Pileser III and Sargon II. What is sure is that Soviet archaeologists have found evidence of ancient Jewish practice in Uzbekistan and what is now Turkmenistan, including a 2,200-year-old synagogue and pottery marked according to Jewish dietary rules.

At the time of Arab conquest of Transoxiana—the area that today includes Uzbekistan, Tajikistan, Kazakhstan, and Kyrgyzstan—in the seventh and eighth centuries, the ethnically intermixed area of present-day Uzbekistan included Zoroastrians, Buddhists, Persian Manicheans, and Assyrian and Miaphysite Christians, all of whom lived side by side. But one by one, these religious communities were almost entirely eradicated through threats of conversion or death, and by the time the Russian Tsars conquered Central Asia, the Jews were the only surviving religious minority.

Under their Muslim masters, the Bukharian Jews were not allowed to build their own houses of prayer, so instead they took to praying at community mosques. It wasn't until the seventeenth century, when community elders made a deal with the grand vizier of Bukhara, that the first synagogue could be built in the city of Bukhara.

But it may have been too little, too late, and for the next century the Jews of Uzbekistan would fall into assimilation. Redemption would end up coming in the form of Rabbi Yosef Maimon, a well-known kabbalist from Safed, who arrived in Uzbekistan on what was supposed to be a short trip, but, upon seeing the sad state of its Jewish community, he decided to stay on as its leader.

Before Maimon's arrival, the Bukharian Jews had used the Saadia Gaon Siddur, compiled and printed in Arabic in 900 BCE, but Maimon taught them Hebrew and introduced them to the traditional Sephardi practices, breathing spiritual life into a community that had been very close to death.

Knowing how many times this community has teetered on the brink of extinction, it makes sense to me that I'm met with almost defensive expressions of observance while we sit around that Kiddush table. When I had gotten up to do the ceremonial washing of my hands before blessing the bread, they scolded me for not waiting until every man was seated and asked me, repeatedly, about my level of religious observance. That's why I'm so surprised to see several members of the minyan break out their phones during and after lunch—something that is strictly prohibited according to orthodox Jewish tradition—and I'm not entirely sure where the line is drawn between ceremony and adherence to Halacha.

The one English-speaker introduces himself as Gavriel. He's a young man, shy yet determined, and the son of one of the community's most impressive figures. Gavriel patiently translates the questions, most of them about my own community and our traditions, and when I tell them that most of Sweden's Jews aren't religious, they shake their heads in disbelief.

"I think it's better to have nothing than to have liberal synagogues and secular Jewish activities," one of the men laments to me.

He's one of two Ashkenazi men who attend the Bukharian synagogue, and he tells me he left his Ashkenazi brethren because they, in his opinion, weren't sufficiently observant.

One would think that he stands out, but the history of Central Asia is reflected in the faces of the Uzbek population, and if there ever were a melting pot, I think this might be it. Some Jews look Persian, others Mongolian, Hazara, or Russian, and most are a mix of all of that, making it impossible to pinpoint the origin of anyone I meet. The difference between the Bukhari and Ashkenazi Jews here isn't visible, but, as I would be told repeatedly throughout the week, it's important to both groups. While many at this lunch started off a sentence by praising the country's all-round unity, they usually ended by saying that theirs is the true expression of Jewish life and one that dates back much further than modern pogroms and European wars.

The man from the Torah reading is looking at me, all throughout lunch, and he does so with a fascinating lack of shyness. I lean into Gavriel and ask about the man that I learn is named Itzak, and he tells me that he is the most learned man in their synagogue, charged with the task of reading from the Torah each week. Itzak is a bit of a mystery, Gavriel tells me, but I had already figured out that much. Divorced, single father, a pious man with the responsibility of an entire synagogue on his shoulders. One of the reasons that Itzak is a mystery to Gavriel is that most of the members of this community don't spend much time together outside of religious holidays and events. Unlike many other small Jewish communities in this part of the world, there are no Jewish neighborhoods or traditional trades, and the Jews work and socialize predominantly outside of their own religious and ethnic groups. This is indicative of a country that has and is doing its utmost to promote national identity before religious identity, and when I ask Gavriel if he misses the community feel of a more closed society, he looks at me with some sort of disbelief.

He answers, "I'm Uzbek. We are Uzbek. That's the number one thing. We are thankful to our government, and we can do whatever we want and get all the support we could wish for, as Jews, as long as we follow the laws of Uzbekistan."

I have heard those words before, in other places, from other Jews, and I tend to be suspicious of any community that goes above and beyond to praise the government that protects it. Usually it means that the freedom they speak of is conditional at best and fictional at worst, but as he says it, I don't know enough about this place to truly judge Gavriel's words on merit. So I just nod and smile and bite into another hard-boiled egg.

I have another appointment to get to, so I excuse myself from the colorful bunch long before I'm ready to go. I make an appointment to meet up with Gavriel after Shabbat, to speak with him and his mother— the community leader—and I leave a stack of my business cards on the table for anyone else who might want to get in touch.

Map in hand, I head toward the Ashkenazi synagogue, where I'm invited for lunch with what I am told are the community elders. I'm calmer now, knowing I won't be late, so I leisurely walk the fifteen minutes through central Tashkent, taking my time to look at the people and places I'm passing.

Tashkent literally means stone village, but with its two and a half million citizens and a vibrant metropolitan feel, it is a village no more. It's not a beautiful city in the traditional sense—no Paris or Istanbul—but it feels alive, exciting, and like a place that is transitioning to something else; reminiscent of when I went with my father to Warsaw in 1992, seeing a country blast through the wall to the West. The architecture is a wild mix of Old Russian low-houses and imposing Soviet structures, and in between them is a solitary shop or two, like an newsstand from the old country, selling round and sweet Uzbek bread.

Tashkent chose to cooperate with the Russians when they arrived in the nineteenth century and ended up becoming the Soviet Union's largest city, a position that is reflected throughout its monuments, parks and broad promenades. That was the first thing I noted when I got here, riding to the city from the airport at two in the morning: how massive the streets are, how everything feels oversized and empty, a typical sign of former Soviet glory.

The Ashkenazi synagogue is housed inside a compound surrounded by a large iron fence that only partially hides a large, stone-clad courtyard where a group of men in their forties have gathered to schmooze. There's no minyan here, other than on the High Holidays, but it still serves as a social hub for the Jews of Tashkent—particularly those of Ashkenazi origin.

Most of the Jews attending this shul have their origin in the countries of the former USSR—from the Ukraine to Poland and Lithuania. Some families arrived here under tsar rule, others as soldiers in the Russian army or fleeing from persecution to the safe haven for Jews that Uzbekistan would ultimately become. Whatever the reason for their arrival, they are proud to be here—that much is clear—and almost as proud to be Ashkenazi.

Dmitri, a tall man with bright eyes and an almost-constant smile, acts as both my host and guide to this part of Jewish Tashkent. He's clearly a *macher* at this shul—one of the big boys—and he introduces me to the gang. From what I can pick up with my rusty Russian, he is not at all displeased to be the one bringing the unexpected guest. Since I can't rely entirely on my high school Russian, I'm relieved when my interpreter Aziz arrives, making us the odd ones out at what feels like a very intimate gathering. Aziz is a Muslim Uzbek, roughly my age, and he throws himself into the conversation with an admirable lack of fear of the elders' suspicious glances.

There's vodka and tea at every table, as seems to be the custom wherever I go. Given that I've already had lunch, I settle for vodka and nibbles, and I lean back to listen to the steady flow of Russian banter that I only barely understand. After a while, Dmitri notices that I'm not exactly engaged, and he offers to show me around. With Aziz by my side, I follow him next door to a well-hidden mini-museum.

Dmitri shows off the treasures of the two-room museum, many of them images of Jewish soldiers who died fighting World War II.

"The Republic killed the fascist machine." That's all he says, while pointing to the names and faces on the wall.

Hundreds of men and women, boys and girls, are looking down at me from the wall. They're somber, most of them dressed in military uniform with rows of metal honors down the front. Dmitri shows me a tattered old book. It says "erythematic" on the front, but as he opens it and turns it over, there's a Jewish book of prayer inside. These books were used under times of Soviet oppression, when the observant Jews had to hide, and for the very same reasons there are five exits to this building—offering many ways to escape for when the KGB came looking for betrayers of communist ideals.

Dmitri has a complicated relationship with this place, with the country itself. Fiercely proud to be an Uzbek, yet referring to himself as Russian from time to time, he saw his own grandparents and parents suffer when they started to question the Bolshevik agenda. Dmitri's maternal grandparents had been true believers, holding high positions within the Communist Party in the 1920s and early 1930s. Then came the great purge, where Joseph Stalin decided to deport ethnic minorities, suppress farmers, and "clean" the Communist party of potential dissidents and saboteurs, many of whom were Jews suspected of dual loyalties.

In 1937, Dmitri's grandparents were charged with treason under Article 58 of the Communist Party statutes and imprisoned without trial. They had given their lives to the cause, and the cause had ultimately taken their lives for the effort. Dmitri shows me a piece of paper dated January 1957, issued by the USSR after the death of Stalin. It's a receipt, of sorts, verifying that Dmitri's grandparents were imprisoned and sentenced to death in 1937 and that they, after further investigation, had been found to be innocent. There is no apology in there, just a statement of facts twenty years too late.

Given the fate of his grandparents and the pain it caused his family, Dmitri knew little to nothing about his Jewish identity while growing up. He matter-of-factly knew he was a Jew, but that fact didn't have any practical or spiritual implications. As the wall came down and the new government promised equal rights to all faiths, Dmitri found his way back to Judaism, learning everything for the first time and slowly reclaiming a legacy and identity that Communism had done its best to eradicate. At forty, he was finally circumcised, and without meaning to, I flinch as he tells me. I erupt into laughter as he does a wobbly dramatization of limping out of the hospital after the procedure.

"I did it late, like Abraham," he says, proudly, and I commend him for his effort, odd as it feels to congratulate a grown man for such a painful ordeal.

Aziz chimes in and asks when Jews are normally circumcised, and his question becomes a welcome distraction to the heaviness of what we just heard, and we chatter about Islam and Judaism for a bit while we walk through the rest of the museum. Before I leave, Dmitri invites me to a Yahrzeit the next day—a memorial ceremony for one of the women in the pictures, the mother of one of the heads of Ashkenazi community.

"You will meet everyone, and there will be *plov* [pilaf], so you can't say no."

So I say yes, and leave the room of memories behind me.

* * *

By the next morning, I'm back to the Bukharian shul, and now the men are *davening* in the smaller study hall, next door to the synagogue. Because there isn't a *mechitze* to divide us, I wait outside while the men finish the morning prayers and watch them through the glass door. There is less collegiality here than I am used to from my own and other communities. No chatter between prayers, no sneaky gossip or schmoozing among friends; just focused and efficient prayer. Once they're done, I ask to take some pictures of the men wearing tefillin, and two of them agree, staring directly into the lens of my camera, proud and unwavering.

I try to smile and coax, but I get nothing, just that look of intensity; and while I don't feel unwelcome, I am somewhat uncomfortable, like a guest who arrived two hours early for the party. Perhaps it is suspicion, perhaps it's a cultural clash, but while I'm there, I become acutely aware of the fact that my bubbly openness is far from universally endearing.

As the *minyan* drops off, Gavriel's mother arrives. She is a force of nature; I know that as soon as she walks in the room. Esther is short in stature, but she fills the room, with a cloud of cigarette smoke and a voice that carries well beyond the walls of the synagogue.

"Did he tell you about Chabad yet?" She asks me.

She grabs a chair and nods at Gavriel who mumbles something inaudible, and Esther goes on to tell me, quite proudly, that she was responsible for kicking out the local rabbi a few years ago.

"He came into our synagogue and pointed out the *mamzerim* (bastards), passing judgment over who was a Jew and who wasn't. These people want to be observant, and when he walked in there and said they weren't even Jews it made them feel like dogs."

Gavriel steps in to give me a diplomatic explanation, something I get a feeling he does a lot, telling me that this is a complicated congregation. Because of the current government's strict policy of Uzbek nationalism trumping religious identity, there has been a lot of intermarriage, and many of the congregants are not *halachically* Jewish. The Uzbek community counts its Jews according to Israel's Law of Return, where one Jewish ancestor is enough. Using that math, there are almost thirty thousand Jews in Uzbekistan. According to Halacha, however, there are about thirteen thousand—eight thousand of whom reside in the capital of Tashkent.

"So," she continued, "I wrote to the government and asked them to have the rabbi removed, and they listened. Now he has his own *shul*, and he is of course welcome here to pray; but he no longer has authority over us or any other Jews in this community."

That's how things are done here, I'm told. The government has final say on all religious affairs, and as long as the Jews comply with their directives, they can rely on the government's support and protection. It's more or less exactly what Gavriel had told me on Shabbat, and it makes me just as uneasy now. I'm curious what she means when she talks about compliancy and what happens when you step out of line, but when I ask, all I get is assurances that this will never be an issue.

"We have zero anti-Semitism here. *Zero.* OK? We are all the same here; Jews, Muslims and Christians, we are all Uzbek, and as long as you are Uzbek first and a law-abiding citizen, the government will protect you."

Every now and then, Gavriel tries to chime in and gets shot down with the loving ferocity that only a Jewish mother can deliver. I could watch them all day, and even when they're arguing in Uzbek I understand what is being said, because I and everyone I know has been cut down that way by our mothers. Esther gets the final word, and Gavriel resigns to making frustrated faces behind her back. When I giggle, Esther shoots me a look that makes my knees tremble, ever so slightly.

She lights another cigarette and leans it against the ashtray while she scribbles something in my notebook—numbers, names and dates, in half-Latin, half-Cyrillic letters.

These are Jewish heroes, she tells me, people who saved and gave lives during World War II, orphans who came here and grew up to be successful Uzbeks, and great rabbis who taught in these halls. She tells me about the Muslims who took in Jewish orphans; who waited for them at the train station and raised them as their own. She tears up as she paints the picture of hardship met with humanity.

She is certainly making the case for her country, and it's impossible not to be moved by the stories of Jewish children taken in by strangers. Yet the story I am most curious about is her own. I wait for her to finish what she quite clearly came here to tell me, and then I dive in.

"But what about you," I ask, "how would you feel if Gavriel marries a non-Jewish woman—do you see a future for him here, raising Jewish children?"

I willfully ignore an uncomfortable Gavriel as I ask this, and I focus on Esther, looking back at me with a charming half-smile.

"We do *giur* (conversion), of course," she replies. "It's easy."

"So, *Halacha* does matter to you," I say, adding, "as it did to the previous local rabbi?"

"We do *our* conversions. I'm not too bothered about if it is a hundred percent accepted by the Israeli rabbinate or not. We do it here. For us."

I clearly overstepped, but I don't regret the question. There is something interesting in the discrepancy between official policy and private choice and the dynamic between outsiders and those in the know. Esther wants Jewish grandchildren, as most Jewish mothers do, and I wonder how much government policy stops her from stating that, outright.

Before Esther leaves for another appointment, she asks me if I have spent time with the Ashkenazim, and when I reply in the affirmative she sighs a little, then leans in.

"We are *one* community. We don't differentiate between Ashkenazi and Sephardi. But I will say that the Ashkenazi synagogue is a rich man's club; they are all about contacts, money and business, and they don't represent Judaism in Uzbekistan."

I'm about to ask her why she feels that way, but she cuts me off while I'm still trying to find the right phrasing.

"Bukharian Jews have been here since The Temple, but someone else is always saying they represent Judaism in Uzbekistan; the Ashkenazim, Chabad…we are the original, but everyone else is always trying to tell us how to be Jews."

And then she leaves, clutching my business card and a packet of Pal Mall slims. I realize I like her. She probably doesn't like me, but I like her, perhaps because she's an amalgam of every woman I have ever loved or ever loved me.

Gavriel and I hang back for a while, looking through old photos and records. I take the opportunity to ask him what I asked his mother, about how he sees his future here and if he hasn't considered moving to Israel while he's still young and unattached?

"How could I leave? My mother is here. She lost a child already, and I could never do that to her. I owe her to stay, and I will. I just couldn't do that to her."

Gavriel loves his mother, and he is a good son. He tells me her story, and I see why she is not only tough but also held in such high regard by those who know her. She had met Gavriel's father while he was fighting for the Red Army in Afghanistan, but it wasn't a love match, right away. Esther had wanted to adopt three Jewish orphans but wasn't allowed to, as a single woman.

"So she wanted a husband to make it happen. Not for herself, but for the kids who needed a mother and a home."

She got her way and adopted Gavriel's three siblings as soon as the ink on the marriage certificate had dried. Gavriel's father, a true gentleman, had known the reasons for the marriage from the beginning, so when enough time had passed, he offered her an out. A year in, he gave her the option to divorce and for him to be on his way, but by then she had fallen for him; and the rest is, as they say, history.

"My father isn't Jewish, and he has said many times that if he knew my mother was a Jew, he would never have accepted her offer."

It's a joke, of course, but I wonder if there's a hint of truth in there and how the gentile had dealt with entering a traditional, Bukharian Jewish world.

But I don't ask, feeling I have already put Gavriel through enough since I got here.

I leave with a book of collected poems that Gavriel lent me for the week. It's an old Bukharian anthology of traditional Persian poetry with Biblical themes, written in Hebrew, in which the unknown authors praise Jewish martyrs killed after refusing to convert to Islam. It feels like the ultimate mixed message, reading those texts after seeing the amount of intermingling that goes on between peoples and religions in this country. Nowadays, such noble acts of defiance are prohibited and unthinkable, yet they're celebrated and remembered as a better time passed.

Once I'm back at my hotel, I flip through the pictures in my camera, drinking coffee and enjoying what seems to be an endless stream of complementary cakes. The hotel is modern and almost completely empty, so the friendly staff hover around me, eager to talk about their own stories of Uzbekistan. They are the new generation of this country, all about twenty to twenty-five years old, and they grab hold of anything Western with both hands, playing out their lives on social media and adopting exaggerated American accents. So every time I hang out at the hotel café, I talk to them, swap stories from their worlds and mine, and they ask my advice on cool captions to add to their Instagram posts. In a few years, they'll probably be fully immersed in the West, and I won't seem the least bit exotic. But for now, I'm a welcome distraction to standing around, and to me, they offer a taste of what it would have been like to grow up here.

When I wake up the next morning, I already have three texts from Dmitri urging me not to be late for the *Yahrzeit* (memorial) service. In the first one, he tells me to be there by ten; in the next, he changes it to nine thirty, verifying the new time in the third one. He's obviously nervous about something, and I write back, trying to ease his mind. He replies within seconds with a large thumbs-up emoji.

I make a point of being forty-five minutes early, and Dmitri looks relieved when I arrive, making a comical curtsy when he sees me up on the synagogue balcony. The *shul* is packed today, and I see plenty of new faces in the crowd, but at the center is the group of middle-aged *machers* that Dmitri had previously introduced me to.

After prayers, Dmitri tells me that it's time to leave for the cemetery, where we will say the mourner's prayer and pay our respects to the fallen. There's a group of us going, about a dozen men and me, and we get into large SUVs and head out of the city. Dmitri and I are riding in a black BMW driven by Michail, the man who is hosting the Yahrzeit. Michail is a large man, in every sense of the word, and I can tell by the way Dmitri acts around him that he is the de facto leader of this group.

Aziz isn't with me this time, and neither of the men speaks any English, so at first, I sit quietly in the back seat while the conversation takes place around me. Then, Michail starts speaking Italian, and because I speak both French and Latin, we're able to carry on a passable conversation.

During the ride, I find out that Michail's family were successful businessmen in the Ukraine who got here well before the War and were able to transfer their businesses and build a fortune in Uzbekistan. Both his parents were soldiers; his father was one of those caught in the siege of Leningrad, losing one of his legs while fighting off the Nazis. His mother, the woman we are honoring today, had come back from war a changed woman, emotionally more than physically, but as women often do, she had continued to carry the family on her shoulders despite the things she had seen.

Once we get to the cemetery, Michail gives a short speech in Russian, and at the end of it, all eyes turn toward me. One of the men leans into me and whispers, "He told us that you are a famous journalist and that we should treat you as such and forget that you are a woman."

There's a double meaning to that statement, and I appreciate them both; I nod to Michail to show that I received his respect and protection. We walk to his mother's grave, an old man recites the *Kaddish* (mourner's prayer), and Michail fights back tears while the *minyan* responds to the words of praise and comfort. It's a brief and beautiful moment, the mid-morning sun streaming through the birch trees, offering a short respite to the biting November cold. There must be thousands of Jewish graves, most of them with pictures or paintings of the deceased, and a few of them feature Hebrew writing. The war is ever-present here; looking at the dates, I see soldier after soldier buried, couples and siblings and sons, names listed next to military rank and accreditation. The Christian, Muslim, and Jewish cemeteries are all side-by-side, and the lines between them are invisible, not unlike the country as a whole. I want to stay longer, but the group is moving toward the cars and the much-awaited *plov*, so I snap a few shots and reluctantly leave with the rest of them, just as the sun leaves the clearing.

* * *

There are four big tables placed to the side of the Ashkenazi synagogue, overflowing with sour-kale salads, sweet bread, and enormous plates of plov, the traditional Uzbek lamb and rice pilaf. I'm seated between Michail and the Israeli ambassador to Uzbekistan, and across from me are two elderly men who enthusiastically refill my glass with vodka every time I take a sip. Dmitri asks me, via an English-speaking translator from further down the long table, how my meeting with the Bukharian

Jews went, and I tell him about Esther, Gavriel, and the impression I had gotten of a very divided community. A debate ensues, all in Russian, and when it finally calms down, Michail tells me that I shouldn't trust the information that Esther has given me.

"Use about three million grains of salt when you listen to her, that's all I have to say. She is just upset that the Ashkenazim are representing the real Jews of Uzbekistan."

I don't say anything back, I just kind of nod and eat my plov while I reflect over the insanity of us always doing this: small communities wrapped up in in-fighting, siding with enemies over brothers because of miniscule differences or territorial claims. My glass keeps being refilled, and because I don't have the stamina of my table companions, I quickly go from tipsy to outright drunk. It's time to leave while I still look professional, and so I thank my hosts profusely before attempting to walk it all off.

During my ten-minute walk, I realize that this is perhaps the first time I have visited a Muslim country without hiding or downplaying my Jewishness in any way. I don't feel scared and exposed walking alone from one place to another. On that first day, with Mahmoud, I had viewed this as an unequivocally good thing, but now, a few days later, I am thinking that the security comes at a cost. The Uzbek government has used strong-arm tactics to minimize differences between religions and create a unified, homogenous people, and it seems to have succeeded. Maybe this isn't as much to provide security for Jews as it is to simply assimilate them?

I spend my last two days in Uzbekistan riding around with Aziz, going to the local bazaars, and shopping for Soviet memorabilia that people bring from their homes and sell in the streets around the city. We get along well and have reached a level of familiarity that allows us to contrast and compare our traditions and faiths, and we even butt heads on some issues. Because he's a gracious and attentive guide, Aziz really wants me to try some of the local delicacies, but since almost all of them contain non-kosher meat, I have to decline his offer. We debate this, over and over, because he just cannot understand why I won't eat *halal* (food permissible under Islamic law), given that the animals are slaughtered in almost identical ways. I tell him that these things matter—big and small rules and intricacies that I myself sometimes don't even understand—and it's obvious that my answer both bewilders and disappoints him. As we go back and forth with the "why won't you just?" and "just because," I realize that the debate we are having in many ways reflects the struggle of the Jewish diaspora.

We are surrounded by the "why won't you just?" question, and the pressure to give in, for either safety, or convenience, or both. Here in Uzbekistan, the Jews have circumvented the question, and, in some ways, the entire debate of who is a Jew and how to remain one, by re-writing the rules and telling people to stay out of their business.

I don't know how well the Jews will fare under the Uzbek model, or if Gavriel will one day have Jewish grandchildren, but I do know why I worry for them and why some of what I saw during this week caused me to pause. The Uzbek government is actively managing and monitoring religious expression and using force to secularize the country, marketing its tactics as modernization and counterterrorism.

Under this rule, religious congregations can exist only under the grace of government approval, a relationship that seems to have many strings attached. This has created a peaceful multi-religious melting pot on one hand, and a slow suffocation of religious expression on the other. Just as under USSR rule, all men are equal, but none are truly free.

CUBA

Luis De Torres, the first Spanish colonialist to set foot in Cuba as part of the discovery of the Americas by Christopher Columbus, was a Jew. De Torres had converted to Catholicism just before he left Spain and arrived in Cuba on November 2nd in 1492, as the first of many converted Jews to arrive in order to colonize the 760-mile-long island for several centuries to come, thus narrowly escaping the Spanish Inquisition.

Throughout its history, the burden of colonialism has weighed heavily on Cuba, having the entire world's superpowers take an interest in the small island and many groups of immigrants seeing it as either a stopover or an opportunity for a fresh start. Well into the nineteenth century, Jews were not allowed to enter former Spanish colonies, and even after the ban was lifted and Jewish immigrants began to settle around Latin America, Jewish legitimacy was still questioned in the eyes of the law. Jews were known to fight assimilation, and in Latin America, historically opposed to religious pluralism, they were looked upon with suspicion and were unwanted as citizens, as they were seen as being disloyal and difficult. Cuba, however, differed from most other Latin American places because the island's indigenous culture had been almost fully eradicated and replaced with immigrants from around the world. This particular Cuban way also expressed itself within the Jewish settlers of Cuba. In other countries,

Jews tended to form "ghettos," living close together and choosing a somewhat common trade. This was not true of Cuba, where Jews lived throughout the island and were found across the entire social and economic spectrums. Cuba's Jewish colony grew to over five thousand by 1924, although it remained in a state of flux for decades to come with thousands arriving and leaving, most commonly to try their luck in the United States after failing to fully adjust. The beautiful island was far from easy to get used to, and especially for Ashkenazic Jews who spoke Yiddish and were used to a Western- or Eastern-European climate, the tropical heat and equally exotic social codes meant a brutal initial adjustment. Sephardic Jews fared better in their new environment. Their Turkish, Portuguese, and Algerian customs and culture were more relatable to the Cubans, and their Ladino language—a mix between ancient Spanish and Hebrew—created a link to their new home that the Yiddish spoken by their Ashkenazi brothers could never provide. Regardless of their origin, most Jewish immigrants started out doing menial jobs as peddlers or workers in garment factories, often with grueling hours and very little pay, but within a decade they had worked their way into the middle class.

After being a Spanish colony for almost four hundred years, Cuba started its road to independence in 1861, when Spain sent several hundred soldiers to control the island and protect the crown jewel in its colonial empire. In 1891, the U.S. intervened and forced Spain out, and soon Cuba was filled not just with American soldiers but government officials as well—all there to help Cuba transition from colony to independent state.

Despite it technically being a military occupation, these were prosperous times for Cuba, seeing their economy grow due to the influx of American investment and the absence of Spanish taxes and tariffs. The interim control of Cuba was ended in 1901 when US President Theodore Roosevelt organized Cuba's first democratic elections, albeit with one single candidate remaining after what turned out to be a tumultuous campaign, and Cuba saw its first democratically elected leader in Tomás Estrada Palma.

Palma's was not a popular nor successful presidency, however, as he was seen as America's candidate, governing under the infamous Platt Amendment to the Cuban constitution, which allowed the United States to intervene unilaterally in Cuban affairs. He was also a part of establishing the American military base in Guantanamo Bay, placing a permanent U.S. presence on the Island. Guantanamo was key in controlling the Caribbean trade and protecting the newly constructed Panama Canal, and once again Cuba felt used by the larger and more powerful international actors, feeling cheated out of their new independence.

There were of course upsides to the international meddling, however. During this time, Cuba started developing its sugar industry, finally capitalizing on its rich natural resource of sugar cane, giving a significant boost to the national economy through the trade with the United States. Because they had lost over five hundred thousand men in their war with Spain, Cuba now had a shortage of workers, making it a haven for migrants looking for a better life. Workers arrived from all over the world—from China to Germany—and ironically, even twenty thousand Spaniards, many of them former fighters in the Cuban-Spanish war, came to seek a better life. One of these men was Ángel Castro, the father of Raúl and Fidel, who ended up working the fields as a day laborer.

In 1906, the U.S. made use of the Platt Amendment and invaded Cuba, claiming that they needed to control the "civil unrest" there, whereas Cubans believed that America wanted to protect its interest in a booming sugar industry. Five years after its independence and the drafting of its first constitution, Cuba was once again in U.S. hands, and the island was now flooded with American investors and businessmen. Several dozen American Jews had been part of the military operation, and some of these decided to stay as part of the occupation army, enjoying the freedom of worship that had been instituted under the U.S. occupation and using it to establish a synagogue—the United Hebrew Congregation. The United Hebrew Congregation held its services in English and followed the religious reform movement, its members being mainly Ashkenazi Jews who had previously immigrated to the U.S. and then moved to Cuba because of its financial opportunities, becoming both affluent and well-respected members of Cuban society. At first, the United Hebrew Congregation also encompassed the Sephardi population, but this attempt at harmony failed as the two Jewish communities were divided from the start, rejecting each other's religious practices and cultural expressions. By 1914, the Sephardim formed their own congregation, Congregacion Union Israelita Chevet Ahim, and as their community grew, they established several branches across the country, from Santiago de Cuba to Havana. The differences between the two groups had many factors: the European Jews (known as *polacos*) identified as culturally and ethnically Jewish, and the Mediterranean Jews (known as *turcos*) were more traditionally religiously observant as well as more affluent, and their children had received Jewish education in their various countries of origin.

Despite the relative hardship of life in the new world, Cuba at this time offered an opportunity for the ambitious and able-bodied to prosper. This was something that the new immigrant Ángel Castro also capitalized on, and within a few years, he had a company that employed over three hundred people. He was a well-connected landowner in Cuba. His and other investors' wealth grew exponentially during World War I, when Cuba's main competitors in the sugar industry were taken out through a halt in shipping and handling of sugar beets. The sugar prices exploded, and Cuba's economy soared, but that surge came to an end alongside the war, when Cubans realized the danger of focusing all its energy on one product in a highly volatile market.

In the 1920s, Cuba was in crisis, with massive poverty and unemployment plaguing the island. The workers, mostly former slaves and immigrants of color, were suffering, whereas the Americans and the white Spanish immigrants they had partnered with were living through the downturn relatively unscathed. This resulted in clashes within society and a vulnerability to the growing threat of communism, something that expressed itself in the election of the protectionist new president, Gerardo Machado. Raising import tariffs and employing masses of poverty-stricken Cubans for government work, mostly rebuilding and revamping Cuba's infrastructure, Machado stabilized the Cuban economy and became a national hero, but what he did not tell his voters was that he was saving Cuba on America's dime. As the great depression took hold of the world, and Cuba was hit with the biggest hurricane in its history, President Machado was forced to pay his debts to U.S. banks by laying off thousands of workers, making severe budget cuts, and enacting new stricter labor laws that reserved government jobs for native-born Cubans. The previously so open and accepting Cuban society turned toward nationalism, and many Jewish immigrants found themselves not only unemployed, but under threat. Despite the unrest, another four thousand Eastern European Jews arrived between 1924–1935, seeking opportunity and safety where there was less and less of it to find, and the Jews were yet again forced to peddle in the streets to stay afloat in their new country. The dire economic circumstances prompted violent public protests, and Gerardo Machado, being a former army colonel, chose to use the Cuban army against his own people, killing several student protestors and causing riots and insurrections against his rule. President Machado soon declared martial law and jailed many of the protestors, creating makeshift courts and public trials. This only fueled the outrage and, in a last-ditch attempt to stay in power, the former anti-imperialist pleaded with the U.S. ambassador for help, but to no avail. The U.S. wanted the ineffective Machado gone, fearing that a standoff between Machado and the up-and-coming soldier Fulgencio Batista could end in all-out war, but any U.S. hopes to calm the waters were soon gone as Batista staged a coup to take over and expel the American troops.

After a dramatic standoff with American forces at the Hotel Nacional in Havana, Batista had managed to declare himself chief of staff of Cuba's army, appointed Ramón Grau President, and forced the U.S. ambassador off the island. Between 1933 and 1935, Cuba changed dramatically, taking many unexpected turns along the way. After his unprecedented coup, Batista worked with Ramón Grau on a comprehensive reform program to bring civil liberties and worker's rights to Cuba. In one hundred days, Cuba had gotten an eight-hour work day, minimum-wage laws, and women's voting rights, and fearing that Communism was on its way to Cuba, the Americans called for a meeting with Fulgencio Batista in an attempt to achieve stability. The meeting bore fruit, as Batista released his former comrade Ramón Grau from all duties in 1934, rolled back some of the more extreme reforms, and became the de facto leader of Cuba, controlling the country through its army. Despite being a dictator, Batista experienced a great deal of popularity, as he was able to balance his close ties to the U.S. with a new and improved constitution in 1940, a document that included land reform, women's suffrage, and a legally established eight-hour workday while excluding the hated Platt Amendment.

The Jewish population followed the Americans' lead and made an effort to create a relationship with Batista, and after it became known that Jews were among the founders of Cuba's communist movement, an official Jewish chamber of commerce was established in order to discard any rumors of Jewish extremism. Anti-Semitism was still just an imported phenomenon, making its way to Cuba by way of Falangists and fascists, but it did not develop roots in what was still a multicultural and heterogenic society. Jews were not granted Cuban citizenship until the late 1930s, but this was not an expression of anti-Semitism. Rather, it was a mix of Cuban suspicion of Jews who tended to be politically left-leaning and active in labor unions and a concession to the U.S. State Department who did not want a slew of Jews seeking asylum in the United States as Cuban citizens. Despite these and other political issues, relations between Cuban Jews and the government were good in the early '30s, something that perhaps can be attributed to the skillful mediation performed by the newly appointed reform rabbi, Meir Lasker, sent to Havana by the Hebrew Union College. Lasker came to be a strong link between the Jews, Batista, and the U.S. Embassy. Zionist sympathies grew during this time across the Jewish-Cuban spectrum, although more prevalently in the Ashkenazi community, as most Zionist writings and meetings were given in Yiddish. There were rallies in support of a Jewish Palestine, funds raised by Zionist organizations such as Keren

Hayesod, and Israeli prime minister Menachem Begin came to Havana to speak for the Zionist cause.

Things became difficult for the Cuban Jews in the mid-1930s when Nazi propaganda hit the shores and started disseminating at an alarming pace in the national media, spreading fear within the community. Opinion pages called for a complete halt on Jewish immigration. Anti-Semitic slurs were being used in national media on a daily basis and quickly becoming commonplace. The historically divided Jewish community failed to meet the challenge of combatting these anti-Jewish sentiments, the Ashkenazi and Sephardi groups refusing to work together; the Sephardim considering the Ashkenazim to be assimilated communists and the Ashkenazim scoffing at the Sephardim's antiquated ways. The result of this lack of cohesion was a community in peril, something that was only exacerbated by the flow of immigrants fleeing Europe as the Nazis tightened their grip on the continent. By 1938, the Jewish population in Cuba had risen to thirteen thousand, ten thousand of which attempted to settle on the island and the rest being in transit.

In May 1939, the MS *St. Louis* arrived at the Havana harbor, carrying with it hundreds of Jewish refugees from Hamburg, Germany. The ship had been destined for the United States, but President Roosevelt had refused to accept the Jewish refugees fleeing Nazi persecution, so they turned back to Cuba in order to plead for asylum there. Negotiators for the ship met with now-President Batista personally, but he asked for such exorbitant amounts of money to accept the refugees that only a handful could pay their way ashore, and over nine hundred Jews were forced to return to Hitler's Germany to meet a certain death. The already-fearful Cuban Jewish population did little to voice its concern for the refugees on the MS *St. Louis*; mindful of the volatility of the situation, they chose to keep a low profile.

American-Cuban friendship lasted throughout the war, and from America's entry in the war, Cuba functioned as an important strategic hub, letting the U.S. make use of the formerly-so-controversial Guantanamo Bay as military storage. To Batista, this was a prosperous friendship, and Cuba saw its economy and military grow in the shadow of the war. Batista's private wealth grew, as well, as he took a cut out of every arms deal made with the Americans. There had always been corruption in Cuba, and a culture of cheating, but now this went from a covert operation to something openly flaunted. Despite having seen its share of popular uprising, the Cuban government paid no heed to the growing rumblings of the lower classes. Fulgencio Batista gave the Italian and Jewish mafias his blessing to build and run casinos and hotels across Cuba, and soon enough, the island paradise had become a haven for money laundering and other exotic extravagances and a refuge for mob bosses that were risking long prison sentences in their home country. The mafia operations in Cuba were under the auspices of Jewish-American mobster Meyer Lansky, a charismatic man who had been brought in by Batista to deal with the widespread cheating at the Cuban casinos. Lansky dealt with it, and he profited greatly from this endeavor, soon creating a form of shadow-rule in Cuba where the political elite and mobsters worked in perfect synchronicity.

The Jewish community reached a level of stability during and after World War II. Many Jewish immigrants either returned to Europe or tried their luck in the U.S., and for those who chose to stay, the linguistic and economic differences between the Jewish groups had been significantly diminished. The Jewish population was now concentrated to Havana, where one could find five synagogues, kosher butcheries, bakeries and restaurants, Jewish schools, and even several daily publications aimed at a Jewish audience. Jews had become a part of the culture, quite literally, and the Jews attempted to re-create their old homelands in Cuba by putting up Yiddish theatre and musical shows and describing their Jewish experiences in poetry and literature. It was not all roses, though, as some of that literature shows. As always, the new immigrants clashed with the old, and there was a significant resentment from those who had been rejected by the United States and now lived in a foreign and bewildering place, seeing some of their Jewish brethren having prospered while they themselves had left with nothing but their lives and the clothes on their backs. There were also cultural clashes when the new immigrants started mixing with the non-Jewish population and, specifically the young women, drew negative attention to themselves and their community. These difficulties showed the need for a more traditional structure within their society, and in the years to come, the community would have established a *bet din*, a Jewish religious court, where both religious and societal issues were arbitrated and solved as well as a system for business management and loans through various international Jewish agencies. In the shadow of the war, the Jews of Cuba grew stronger, and before the end of the war the first group of second-generation Jewish immigrants graduated from the University of Havana. Slowly but surely, and despite much hardship, the exotic island had become a home.

Meanwhile, the poor in Cuba were becoming poorer by the day, and by 1947 there were six hundred thousand unemployed Cubans out of a population of seven million. At this time, Ángel Castro's illegitimate child, Fidel Castro, was a politically engaged law student at the University of Havana. Having already fought on the side of revolutionaries in both Colombia and the Dominican Republic, Fidel had made quite a name for himself as an outspoken rebel, and once he graduated from university, Fidel spent his days doing pro bono work for the poor. There were opposing powers at work in Cuba in the early '50s, and the clash was inevitable. On the one hand, Fulgencio Batista, bankrolled by Meyer Lansky, planned to take back power from the once-again-powerless President Grau. On the other hand was a growing Communist undertow, led by Fidel Castro, his brother Raúl, and an army of their closest men. By 1952, Batista realized he could never win a democratic election, so rather than risking defeat, he took back power through a military coup and started ruling Cuba through dictatorship. Army general Batista, now a multi-millionaire, ignored the constitution he himself had once so proudly written and instituted, and soon democracy had been exchanged for brutality, extrajudicial executions, and mass jailings. After a failed attack on Cuba's biggest military barracks, Fidel Castro was arrested by Batista's army and put on trial, where he was sentenced to fifteen years in prison for his attempt to overthrow the government. Fidel and Raúl Castro, along with members of their revolutionary group, received a political pardon in 1955 and vowed to go to Mexico to plan a new revolution in the name of what was now called "The 26th of July Movement." While in Mexico, the Castro brothers befriended the Argentinian physician and revolutionary Che Guevara as well as members of the KGB and, with new alliances and financial reinforcements, a group of eighty-two revolutionaries finally returned to Cuba to finish what they had started a few years before.

After a failed initial attempt at a revolution, the Castro brothers, Che Guevara, and a significantly decimated band of comrades hid out in the Cuban jungle, attempting to regroup. This could have failed, had not an American journalist from the *New York Times* been smuggled into the camp, leading to a three-part series on Fidel Castro and the romance of the people's revolution. The articles painted a picture of a Robin Hood of the Caribbean, and described Fidel as being friendly to the U.S. and in favor of a democratic revolution—with the sole goal of removing an evil dictator. This exposure resulted in a flow of new recruits and a strengthened sense of purpose to the 26th of July Movement; and it also was the first of many propaganda-victories for commander Fidel.

By 1958, as sympathies for the "romantic revolutionary" grew across the world, the U.S. government stopped all weapons shipments to Cuba and thereby left Batista unsupported, and Fidel Castro saw the chance to make his move. Fulgencio Batista fled on New Year's Eve in 1958, and by January 1st, 1959, the Cuban state collapsed, and Fidel could enter Havana in victory.

After years of frustration, humiliation, and corruption, the Cuban people hoped for a new day under Fidel Castro, but they soon saw the freedom and democracy he had spoken of be replaced by the same dictatorship and oppression they knew—only this time all the power emanated from one single source: El Comandante. Immediately after naming himself Prime Minister, Castro set up revolutionary courts that led to the execution of at least three thousand people, and, together with his brother Raúl and newly appointed Finance Minister Ernesto "Che" Guevara, he started the process of expropriating private companies in

Cuba, resulting in thousands of landowners and business owners fleeing the country with whatever they were allowed to bring.

From that point on, Cuba and Castro started severing ties with the U.S. while embracing the Soviet Union, causing tensions not only with the Eisenhower administration but with the rest of the world. After a failed operation at the Bay of Pigs, led by the newly elected and highly reluctant President Kennedy, Fidel Castro was able to secure his position and give legitimacy to the revolution that it otherwise would never have achieved. Now fully in bed with Moscow, Castro declared the revolution, and Cuba, to be socialist. This was a fast and dangerous leap for the revolutionary who, during his coup against Fulgencio Batista, claimed to not be a communist but rather a fighter in the name of human rights and democratic values.

The situation for the island's Jews started deteriorating, as religion was now deemed opium for the people, and survival took precedence over observance. Ninety percent of the Jewish population left the island, and although synagogues stayed open and untouched, Jewish Cuba was in fast decline. Castro's revolution was a hard blow for Cuba's Jews who had become successful and prosperous, and because of their relative wealth, they were some of the first to be targeted for nationalization and expropriation. Another reason that the Jews were quick to leave Cuba during and after the revolution was that they had previous experience of persecution from their countries of origin, and the rhetoric emanating from the Castro camp was eerily familiar, prompting them to look elsewhere, leaving all that they'd accumulated behind. The Jews made new homes in the U.S., most of them ending up in Florida, forced to be immigrants once again.

* * *

Arriving in modern-day Cuba is a curious thing, as it is as much time travel as tourism, something that is evident as soon as you set foot in the airport. Clad in what once was a happy green coat of paint, it is both desolate and bustling, and the faint smell of mold is ever-present there, as throughout the island. I arrive a mere month after the death of Fidel

Castro, but little has changed since the departure of the founder of the revolution. The regime is now taking orders from Fidel's brother Raúl, with its infamous security service, *Dirección General de Inteligencia* (DGI) making sure the wheels turn smoothly. It is a simple yet brilliant scheme, where every neighborhood has an informant, reporting to the *Comités de Defensa de la Revolución* (CDR), a secret police in charge of keeping tabs on counter-revolutionary activity, and every infraction or sign of disloyalty is met with stern and immediate consequences. Given the dire straits of the people in Cuba, the regime is not willing to take any chances; having experienced revolutions in the past, it knows not to allow the flame of change to be ignited.

With a monthly salary of thirty U.S. dollars per person, supplemented with a fixed portion of rice, eggs, and beans, the people of Cuba have been forced to use every opportunity to make some money on the side in order to avoid starvation. This has resulted in a shadow society to take shape within Communist Cuba, a society that is highly capitalist, in every single way. I get evidence of this on route to old Havana one day, when my driver stops for gas and is told there is none left, only to leave the car with a fistful of cash and return later, car filled up and ready.

"This is what we call the Cuban way. You see, the gas station belongs to the government, so the only way for these men to earn something extra is to sell gas to the highest bidder and deny those who can't pay. I call it Communist capitalism."

The same is true everywhere you go, people cooking the books to fill their plates and fight their way out of desperation, and as a tourist you accept it and move on, constantly struggling with the guilt of living here in a bubble that everyday Cubans will never be privy to. To outsiders, the combination of poverty and oppression and the recent loss of the symbol of the revolution would inevitably result in turn toward democracy and capitalism, but, as the regime does its best to convey, very little has been buried with Fidel.

The Cubans I have spoken to are proud of their country, and even though they criticize the regime, under promise of anonymity, they are quick to add that they don't necessarily want Cuba to become the U.S.

or just any other country in the West. When I ask them if they believe that democracy and capitalism will come to Cuba now that Fidel has left and Raúl is on his way out, they respond in the negative, saying that whatever will come next will be a Cuban version of those things, an adaptation from what is now.

And the way things are looking, they may be right. Rumor has it, Raúl Castro has already reshuffled the government, replacing generals and ministers with his personal confidants so that he will remain the unofficial leader even after his assumed successor, Miguel Díaz-Canel, is sworn in as President in 2018. This ensures that even though Fidel is dead, the spirit of the revolution lives on, and the Cubans I've spoken to fear that the regime will take steps to emphasize the status quo by tightening its grip on the population. It is not an improbable scenario but rather a common tactic for totalitarian regimes when dealing with dramatic shifts, as most recently seen in Iran after the deal, where executions and imprisonments have risen dramatically during and after the rapprochement with the West. There is an important difference, however, and that is that Cuba is unlike many other countries of its kind, and that difference may actually be a hindrance in its journey toward democracy.

One thing that sets Cuba apart from other totalitarian regimes is the romance that surrounds it, still, despite the thousands of extrajudicial executions and arbitrary imprisonments, a ruined national economy, and denial of basic freedoms of association, religion, movement, and speech having taken place in the past fifty-eight years. Even those who do not hold an ideological torch for the Communist revolution are still enchanted with the country's beauty, charm, and lust for life, making it easier to disregard the daily crimes committed against its people and to quell the international community's instinct to intervene. Cuba is truly magical, and yes, it is full of life, but once you step outside of the lush hotel garden, you see that it is life on the brink of death—magic existing in a state of suspended animation.

Life inside the Jewish community is a reminder of that state, and of the larger problems plaguing the country that holds it. The Orthodox synagogue, Adat Israel, is placed inside the colorful Old Havana neighborhood and could easily be missed in the intensity of its daily hustle. Set inside a dark building, two stairs down, I enter the synagogue on a hot and humid Thursday afternoon, and the pews are filled with tourists who are eagerly listening to Avraham, the ad hoc interim rabbi, who despite his impressive stature speaks in a surprisingly docile tone.

He tells what looks like a predominantly American Jewish audience that the community consists of mainly seniors, and that an aging population is a major issue in Cuba generally, not only within the Jewish community; and that since they receive no help from the Cuban government, the community lives off charity given by tourists. The group gets the not-too-subtle hint and reaches for their wallets as they leave, and I ask the man if the lifting of sanctions has helped the Jews of Cuba and given them more visitors and more charity, giving them a better quality of life?

"Quite the contrary, actually. With sanctions in place, people had to apply to come specifically here, specifically to visit the Jewish community, and that way we were guaranteed a certain amount of people each year. Nowadays people want to do the tourist thing, and they stop by the synagogue for a moment, but the specific Jewish tourism is not as popular anymore."

The community was, for all intents and purposes, dead between 1960 and 1990, but it experienced a rebirth after the fall of the Soviet Union. After that point, it became possible to practice religion again, but doing so would still create a schism between you and the rest of Cuban society. As a Jew, you have to register as religious, and one of the reasons people do, despite tensions, is that there are some upsides for the members in being registered, as members receive certain benefits from the Jewish community. With every attempt at registration, the heads of the community check the Jewish background of their members, and Cuba is a small enough place to verify a person's Jewish bona fides, using either word of mouth or a simple trip to the cemetery. Despite the dwindling Jewish population, the community has not conceded to any liberal measurements of Jewishness, still measuring Jewishness according to Halacha without exception.

As do most Jewish communities in the Diaspora, Cuba's suffers from assimilation; with an intermarriage rate of ninety-seven percent, the decline is both swift and unrelenting. What differs from other Diaspora communities is that the assimilation is not related to anti-Semitism, as that is not an issue in Cuba, nor has it been in any significant way through history. The Jews try to keep kosher, but being strictly kosher is of course very difficult, as Cuba is very politically and geographically isolated. In a way, people keep kosher out of necessity more than anything else, as they cannot afford to buy *treif,* and meat isn't available to people, generally, but rather given to the fancy hotels to cater to tourists and higher-ups. The very special circumstances of Cuban life are reflected in Cuban Jewish observance, as well. Not that the community isn't observant, to the extent it can be, but rather that it makes concessions due to the dire political and financial situation, such as eating guava rather than apples on Rosh Hashana because apples are not available. As for the day-to-day, most of the weekly activities in and outside of the synagogue are non-religious in nature, and that is another expression of the difficulties plaguing the country. These activities are upkeep and practical things such as killing mosquitos in the synagogue and arguing with government over trash piling up in the street and becoming a health hazard.

A positive side effect of the situation in Cuba is that there are no divisions between Jews on the island. Everyone within the community interacts on a weekly basis, and people will go to two services on Shabbat in order to receive two much-needed meals. As Avraham tells me in his laconic way, "In Cuba, you have to attract people with a mechanism, and the best mechanism is food."

As for the relationship between Jews and other religious groups in Cuba, Avraham says that is an uncomplicated affair.

"Cuban Newspapers have fewer than five pages, so we have no space for news of the conflict, and the island has stayed insulated; and that can perhaps explain the lack of anti-Semitism."

Cuba is an island in every sense of the word, and Cuban Jews are islanders, with a unique character and outlook. With no common ancestry, they share the place they ended up in, and they have grown accustomed to the ebbs and flows of life as Caribbean Jews. The ability to adapt has kept the Jews alive all over the world for centuries, but that ability can also prove fatal when the adaptation drives them too far from their roots.

Avraham has a wife and two young children, and he dreams of making Aliyah one day. For now, he stays because he feels responsible for the community; he is the only one reading from the Torah and who has the necessary knowledge, practical and theoretical, to keep the Havana community afloat.

As of 2017, there are approximately fifteen hundred Jews in Cuba, over one thousand of them residing in Havana, where there are three somewhat active synagogues: El Patronato (Ashkenazi and Conservative) synagogue and community center, Centro Hebreo Sefaradi (Sephardi and Conservative), and the aforementioned Adat Israel. The remaining four hundred Jews are spread out across the Island, the two biggest clusters outside of Havana being in Santa Clara, the capital city of the central Villa Clara province, and the city of Cienfuegos, on the far-southern coast. These two cities house communities of eighteen and nineteen Jews respectively, and while their effort to keep Jewish life alive in these places is admirable, the numbers are dwindling quickly; and as the Jewish tourism remains focused on Havana, it makes fundraising difficult and Jewish life around the island an isolated affair.

Looking at Cuban Jewish life, the question arises whether or not it is in their interest to sustain it, or if it has become a cause for the more affluent and lively Diaspora? To anyone looking at the Cuban Jews, the pain and poverty is evident, and one wonders if there is a point where it is time to shut the door. It is in these communities, the ones on the brink of extinction, where the value of Diaspora life is truly put to the test. With a handful of Jews left and very little in terms of Jewish infrastructure, they run the imminent risk of becoming symbols rather than individuals, and while they could be living better Jewish lives in Israel— would they choose to—they have come to represent some form of hope that goes above and beyond their individual lives. This larger responsibility is something that, for cultural, religious, and historical reasons, is built into the Jewish psyche, and few places is this more visible than in the isolated island of Cuba. Avraham stays in Cuba. Not for himself, but for the other Jews, and—in a larger sense—the entire Jewish world. It is a moving concept, yes, but a worrying one, and it begs the question if dying in honorable dignity trumps the instinct to leave and to survive.

Cuba is stuck in between its significant ties to the Holocaust and a government whose political interests make them downplay the atrocities or use them to make political points. Most recently, after a moment of silence for Holocaust victims during a 2017 UNESCO summit, Cuba called for a moment of silence for Palestinians, thereby equating the two and implying the Israelis were perpetrating genocide against the Palestinians. The icy relationship between the Cuban and Israeli governments along with the Communist restriction on religion has placed the Cuban Jews in a difficult position, as they have little left on which to hang their Jewish identity.

Cuba is also an example of what happens if both Zionism and religion are taken out of play and both lines of contact are interrupted. Although the relationship between Israel and Cuba has improved since Fidel Castro attacked Israel in the UN in 1979, accusing Israel of committing "the most terrible crime of our era" against the Palestinians in front of the UN's General Assembly, leading to the Israeli envoy calling him "an enemy of Israel," there are still no diplomatic relations, and the relationship is icy, at best. The animosity toward Israel, in combination with the previous ban on religious practices, has left the Jewish community of Cuba untethered, and as a result the community is all but lost. Those who make Aliyah at this point do so in order to escape the socioeconomic plights of Cuba and start over in a country where they know they will be welcomed.

MOROCCO

I arrive in Marrakesh the day before Passover, traveling there on equal measures of whim and mission. It is my first time in North Africa, and despite considering myself a woman of the world, the culture shock is quite pervasive. The heat notwithstanding, the chaos is different than others I have seen in the Arab world, and the ancient city streets hold as many mules as cars, carrying everything from people to spices and other precious cargo.

I have been invited for Passover Seder in the Lazama Synagogue, built in 1492 and now housed inside a sixteenth-century *riad* in the Mellah. There used to be twenty-five to thirty synagogues in the Mellah, but now Lazama—a name derived from "Al Azma," meaning "those who ran away"—stands alone as a blue and white mirage in an otherwise dusty and destitute part of the city. I arrive early, as always, to what will be my home for the first two days of the festival, and as I walk down the narrow alleyway toward the synagogue, people are lining up, volunteering to show me the way. Outside the ornate iron door there is a single policeman who greets me with a smile, and what I see inside could not be a more dramatic break from the chaos outside.

Jewish and Muslim life in Morocco are often described as intertwined, the two groups having lived so close to each other through most of history. This is a truth with caveats, as Jewish life for the most part has been limited to restricted areas, or ghettos, but these ghettos have worked as both limiting and protective factors, helping keep Jews Jewish through sometimes very difficult circumstances in the Muslim country.

What we know for sure is that Jewish life in Morocco is of ancient origin, and Hebrew writing found in Fez has been dated back to before Roman times. Up until the fifth century, Jewish Berbers lived alongside their non-Jewish counterparts and did so safely, by all known accounts, and the calm lasted for another two hundred years, at which point the Arab Muslim invaders came and brought with them the choices of conversion, flight, or death for the Jewish Berber tribes.

The Jews who survived relocated to the mountains or the desert and went from gathered to scattered throughout the land, a period of displacement that lasted until the arrival of Emir Idris II, son of the founder of the famous Idrisid Dynasty and a respected scholar and thinker of his time. Idris II ruled Morocco during much of the eighth century, and during his rule, the country opened up to and even welcomed Jewish settlers in the land. The era of intellectualism and openness started by Emir Idris led to veritable glory days for Jewish life in Morocco, and great Jewish minds from Alfasi to Maimonides came to live in Morocco for periods of time, making it a hub for Jewish thought and religious life.

However, the heyday turned hellish by the twelfth century, as the Almohad Caliphate, a religious movement of Muslim Berber origin that had grandiose ideas of religious reformation, replaced the Idrisid Dynasty and re-established Marrakesh as a center of religious and political power. Under the Almohad rule, Jews were forced to wear identification stating their cultural and religious belonging, and Jewish *mellahs* (ghettos) were built in order to contain the Jewish population. By the late 1800s, all of the country's Jews were living in mellahs, and little was left of the respect and co-existence they had known under the Idrisid era.

The modern-age Mellah courtyard is serene, and I stand there, just looking, for almost ten minutes. It is my first meeting with the Moroccan *riad*, a building turned inward toward a courtyard, and the open architecture and the colorful mosaic covering the entire building fascinate me; new things keep catching my eye. I am interrupted in my gaze by my host, Hannah, a British woman who had come here many years ago and made a family, and together we go upstairs to prepare for the meal and await the arrival of more travelers from all across the globe.

While we put the bowls and bottles in their places, the men gather for the prayers on the floor below us. It's a familiar chatter in the court-yard, and were it not for the oppressive heat I could be walking toward my own house of prayer on the streets of Stockholm. Once I am in, I see the subtle but delightful differences. I know the words but struggle with the pace and order, frantically flipping through my prayer-book to find my bearings. Suddenly the men stop, they argue in Arabic, loudly, and I giggle up on my balcony as I realize they too are disagreeing on the how and when. It's like home, though faraway and exotic, and I am with family though I may not know their names. In that I take comfort and decide not to struggle; instead I lean back and listen to the well-known and unfamiliar tunes.

Morocco never managed to purge itself of its Jews, despite the continuous hardship they encountered under the hand of the politi-cal and religious leadership. More Jews kept arriving as life elsewhere became harder yet, and the most significant influx of Jews came from Spain and Portugal as these countries began their persecution of the Jewish minority. For seven centuries, from the seventh to the fifteenth, the Jewish population of Morocco grew thanks to these *m'gorashim* (refugees), and the newcomers settled in the coastal area of the country. Due to barriers built by language and culture, the native Jews did not mix with the refugees initially.

Although legally considered *dhimmis* or "humbled" second-class citizens, the Jews of Morocco gained access to all levels of society, and the m'gorashim did particularly well when it came to bettering them-selves in their new country. Because of their diverse cultural and lingual skills and academic learning, members of the Jewish community would come to serve as ambassadors to European countries, were appointed to the higher courts, and became members of the intellectual elite. By the mid-1600s, the m'gorashim had fully immersed themselves in the indigenous Jewish community, and a new Jewish language started taking shape in Morocco, where Spanish was mixed with Hebrew and Arabic.

As the Jews started becoming more visible throughout society, they also became further victimized. Still forced to wear visible identifiers and burdened by punitive taxation, their lives may have been stable but far from safe. Under Sultan Mulay al-Yazid, serving from the mid- to late-1700s, hundreds of Jews were massacred as punishment for a business deal gone wrong, and this form of collective punishment was far from unusual. Throughout the twentieth century, the Jewish population was subjected to bouts of violence, yet they kept advancing in society. Some of this advancement can be attributed to the relative protection the French imperial power and eventual protectorate over Morocco afforded them. The protectorate, established through the treaty of Fez in 1912 and lasting until Moroccan independence in 1955, helped westernize Morocco, but as in many other cases, the Western values came with a side of assimilation.

While the Jews were still speaking the traditional Judeo-Arabic language and educating their children through *cheders*, Muslim tradition had bled heavily into Jewish life, and a clear expression of that amalgam was the way Jews adopted Muslim mysticism and superstition. Still stuck in the cramped mellahs, disease spread quickly, and death tolls were high due to horrible living conditions. The Jews of the mellah blamed this on the "jinn," the evil eye, and took precautions to ward off their misfortune. From worshipping the same saints to mystic rituals and use of the five-finger *hamsa*, the Jews had adopted the ways of their Muslim and Berber neighbors, but the acts of benevolence were merely tolerated and not reciprocated. The Jews continued to keep themselves to themselves, and life in the mellahs was not as much a result of comfort as of security; in the mellah they could run their businesses and lives with a level of control and avoid the possible threat the outside still posed to them.

Being far away from home on Passover is a strange thing for a Jew. This is a holiday focused on family and remembrance, and being so far from home can make one feel a bit lost. The people around the table are from Morocco, Sweden, Britain, and America, and we are all both lost and home in every sense of those words as we gather in the Mellah on this auspicious night. Our host is guiding us through the story of the exodus from Egypt while explaining the specific Moroccan details of the seder, such as holding the seder-plate over each guest's head while making the traditional Arabic ululation, the high-pitched tongue-trill heard on celebratory occasions in the Middle East. After so many years in Morocco, she performs the act perfectly and tells us that this will bring fortune and good luck. The almost mournful howl echoes between the walls of the riad, and, together with my host's colorful kaftan, it beautifully summarizes the eclectic mix that is Jewish Morocco.

The meal lasts until the early hours of the morning, and just before dawn, my host and I walk one of the other women home through the maze-like Mellah. Walking there, I see how protected we were on the inside, the realities of the outside coming at us, clear and stark. As much as I try, I cannot help but shudder at the howls and comments directed at our hurrying group. My host is dressed very modestly, but I am wearing what I would anywhere else. I soon realize that had I lived here, I would adapt my life to avoid the scene I'm seeing. I would make concessions to the society I lived in, just in order to stay safe.

Ironically, because she is identified as a Jew, my host is safer than others would be walking through this area at four in the morning. She tells me that Jews are considered mystical and are somewhat revered, and for a long time Muslims were afraid to even walk into a synagogue or a Jewish establishment. The protection from the king means a great deal, and the people of Morocco know that Jews are in good standing; therefore it would be more costly to harm a Jew than to hurt another, and classic stereotypes such as Jews being rich and prosperous have resulted in a certain respect being shown toward Jewish individuals. Hannah lives in the Mellah as a highly visible Jew, in some ways *the* visible Jew, and therefore she represents the entire community—a tall order for such a small and humble woman. Many people before her have crossed oceans for love and started new lives in faraway lands, but for Hannah that meant not only a geographical shift but also a not-insignificant change in behavior and circumstance. Hannah is known by name everywhere we go, and I can tell how the people of the Mellah keep a respectful distance from her as she walks by. It strikes me as both a sign of honor and a shield of loneliness, all at once, and I cannot help but wonder what it feels like to be responsible for walking the fine line between two peoples—one's very presence being an act of mediation.

The relationship between Jews and Muslims in Morocco is described in Norman Stillman's "Muslims and Jews in Morocco" (*Jerusalem Quarterly*, 1977) as a form of separate but equal. According to Stillman, "Most of the Moroccan stereotypes of Jews may be negative, but they are also peripheral. They [Jews] are considered dhimmis, humbled but protected subjects. As long as the Jew conforms to this role, he arouses little interest." Stillman goes on to say that despite this, there was a certain "pull" for the Jews to convert to Islam, given the financial and societal ramifications of their Jewishness.

The tribulations were described and lamented in Arabic-style poems called *qasidah*s, and these monorhymed Hebrew poems in Arabic meters were usually performed by women and passed down through generations as a way of transmitting history and emotion. These oral pieces of history were a way of dealing with major issues in the lives of Moroccan Jews and greater historical events, such as violence, religion, and the dream of a life in Israel.

Despite the sometime precarious existence of Moroccan Jewry, the very nature of Morocco was a saving grace during World War II, when the French-appointed Sultan Mohammed V made sure that Moroccan Jews did not meet the same fate as the approximately four thousand North-African Jews that were murdered in the Holocaust. Journalist Richard Hurowitz told the story of the saved Moroccan Jews in his 2017 *LA Times* piece on the topic, in his op-ed "You must remember this: Sultan Mohammed V protected the Jews of Casablanca":

When Paris fell to the Germans in July 1940, the sultan, then 30, was put in a precarious position as Morocco came under the rule of the collaborationist French Vichy regime. Among their first acts,

*the new overseers sought to impose anti-Semitic laws in Morocco.
Jews had lived in that part of the world since well before Carthage
fell, and over a quarter-million called Morocco their home in
1940. Members of the community had served the sultans' court as
ministers, diplomats, and advisers. Mohammed V took seriously his
role as Commander of the Faithful, which he viewed to include all
"people of the book," meaning everyone belonging to the Abrahamic
faiths—Jews, Christians, and Muslims…"There are no Jews in
Morocco," he declared. "There are only Moroccan subjects."*

The experience during the Holocaust shows not only the very special
relationship between the Muslims and the Jews in Morocco, but also
how the role as a "subject" rather than a citizen came to protect the Jews
from harm in a very dangerous time. No Moroccan Jews were deported
or killed during the war, nor were they forced to wear yellow stars as
identifiers, and when the Jewish State of Israel was founded in 1948, the
king once again came to the aid of the country's Jews when the rest of
the Arab world was exploding in angry protest over the historic decision. This truly heroic act on the part of the king—standing up against
first the Vichy regime and later the greater Arab world—would play a
big role in the fate of his Jewish subjects down the line. The very special
relationship between Jews and Muslims in Morocco can also be seen in
the expressions of Holocaust remembrance and how, during its Holocaust Remembrance Conference in 2011, the prestigious Al-Akhawayn
University honored Morocco's late King Mohammed V, who refused to
hand over Morocco's Jewish population to the French Vichy regime. The
late king's actions are a point of pride for the country, and his legacy is
used to educate Moroccans on the events of the Holocaust and keep the
memory of both the atrocities perpetrated against Moroccan Jews and
the heroic acts of Moroccan Muslims alive.

By the mid-twentieth century, Jewish life in Morocco started changing as the Jews started to relocate, moving from the Atlas Mountains
and the desert towns toward the big cities, such as Casablanca and
Marrakesh. At first it was the young who picked up and left, but as the
youth trickled out of these small and medium-sized communities, they

ended up dying out entirely. By the mid-1950s, twenty-five thousand Jews had been added to the Jewish communities of Casablanca, Fez, and Marrakesh.

The big cities were already overcrowded, and the mellahs even more so, and the population-peak had disastrous results for public health. In 1952, half of all Jewish children in Casablanca died before reaching their teens, and disease spread quickly between the narrow and overpopulated houses, leading to many deaths of otherwise preventable diseases. The economic situation was also dire, ninety percent of the Jews were considered impoverished by the early 1950s, and, as the main focus in Jewish Morocco was on survival, observance and tradition gave way to the everyday strife.

As independence from France was drawing closer, Moroccan Jews feared that they would be victims of violence from the Muslim population, and they set their sights on the newly founded Jewish state. Approximately thirty-five thousand Moroccan Jews arrived in Israel between 1948 and 1956, assisted by the Jewish Agency of Israel, using makeshift refugee camps in Casablanca as a hub for the massive effort. The covert Aliyah of Moroccan Jews to Israel continued even after the Moroccan independence in 1956, and between 1956-1961, another thirty thousand Jews arrived in Israel. The most dramatic and well-known part of the Moroccan Aliyah is the tragedy of the ship *Egoz*, a ship that was secretly bringing forty-four Jews from Morocco. The *Egoz* sank on January 10–11, 1961 on its way from Casablanca to Gibraltar (where the refugees would go on to Israel), taking the lives of the Jewish refugees and two crewmembers. The event caught the world's eye, and suddenly the fate of Moroccan Jews was becoming a cause for Jews and non-Jews alike, helping to put pressure on the Moroccan king Hassan II to not allow but at least ignore the Aliyah that continued on until 1964. By 1965, two hundred and fifty thousand Jews had made Aliyah from Morocco to Israel, and they are to date the largest group of immigrants from an Arab country.

Moroccan Jewry shares some commonalities with other Jewish communities within Muslim countries that I have visited in that there is a sense of freedom with strings attached and a permanent state of exception that is uncomfortable and odd. Loyalty to the king and the state is a given, and being a Jew here is always prefaced by the word "Moroccan" as to make sure one understands the special circumstances that these words entail. Moroccan Jews are the chosen minority, and as such, they are important to the kingdom as proof of openness and acceptance; but they are by no means equal to the Muslims—sometimes for the better but most of the time for the worse.

One could say that Jews that live anywhere outside of Israel are beholden to their hosts and to the state that they inhabit, but there are shades of grey within that truth that become stark in contrast with countries like Morocco. The Moroccan Jews are thankful for the protection of the king because here, they *need* protection, and these factors create a symbiotic and co-dependent relationship that one would assume could influence the very nature of Jewish life and its expressions in Morocco.

I meet with Joseph the day before I leave Morocco, at a hotel just on the outskirts of town. Joseph moved from the U.S. to Morocco twenty years ago, for love, and since then he has worked with an organization promoting Muslim-Jewish relations. The work entails helping Muslim youth and families both financially and through educational efforts and, according to Joseph, this will slowly but surely change how Muslims view Jews. He believes that the relationship between the two groups in Morocco can work as a model for the rest of the Middle East.

"What we have here is a functioning relationship, and we live close, like family. There are no attacks on Jews, no violence," he tells me.

Joseph is right in that there have been no attacks toward Moroccan Jewry, and Moroccan Jewry has a special place within the Arab world, as Morocco seems shielded from some of the geopolitical turbulence that otherwise defines the region. But, as I am curious about what that functioning relationship actually entails, I ask Joseph if he thinks the work he does is about creating an equal partnership between Muslims and Jews or if these are measures taken to gain acceptance by the Muslims in their country. Joseph pauses and looks at me.

"Are we equals? No. But this relationship we are building here, what we are doing for these families, that will trickle down through generations and perhaps create equality, down the line."

It's easy to dismiss that work—or the Jewish life in Morocco—as subservience toward the Muslim community, but perhaps it is important to put it into a larger perspective. Jews in Morocco have created a singular world, seemingly far from both the wider Jewish and Arab contexts. Their lives and beliefs float and mix and intertwine, and therefore it is very difficult to speak to the quality of Jewish life when it compares to few others, if any at all.

Any Jewish life outside of Israel is, in one way or another, forced to be a quieter one—a life of adaptation—and Moroccan Jews have a long tradition of living just that way. The work that Joseph, and many like him, do is focused on Jewish survival in North Africa and is based on a mutually beneficial relationship where Jews will be if not equal, then accepted because they show an amount of generosity and goodwill. One might see that as a form of pandering or even humiliation, but one might also say that this is a realistic way forward for Jews to find safe haven in a Muslim community and to allow these ancient communities to survive—understanding that relative equality may be secondary to full protection.

IRAN [1,2,3]

It's 4:00 a.m. and the departure hall in Istanbul's Atatürk Airport is crowded and humid, bustling with activity. I've resigned to sit on the floor with my cup of hot tea, bought mostly to occupy my hands that are shaking with nervous excitement.

Three months prior to my midnight arrival in Istanbul, I decided to apply for a journalist visa to go to Iran, never thinking it would really come to pass. I had a dream to visit one of the most elusive Jewish communities in the world, to get behind the veil of this ancient culture, but through all the arduous paperwork and embassy interviews that pushed the process forward, I kept the reality of entering Iran far from my mind.

Persian Jewry dates back over twenty-seven thousand years, from before the Persian Empire in 539 BC when Cyrus the Great captured Babylon, but despite this proud ancestry, the Jews of Iran remain isolated and, to a large extent, unknown to the rest of the world.

At its height, just ahead of the Islamic revolution, the Jewish community in Iran consisted of approximately eighty thousand individuals. They were thriving in the Persian pearl, being overwhelmingly middle or upper-middle class. Jews boasted a wide array of learning and cultural institutions alongside at least thirty active synagogues in Tehran alone. While the ancient Jewish community had been growing steadily under the protection of the shah, the dawn of the Islamic Revolution brought on a mass exodus of Jews from Iran, reducing the community to just a tenth of its original size.

The advantages the Jews had experienced under the rule of the shah—high socioeconomic status; strong ties to Israel and the United States—became liabilities in the age of the Ayatollah Khomeini.

As with many other dark eras in Jewish history, the Jews were accused of stealing the country's treasures. Flyers circulated throughout Tehran urging vengeance against the Jews. There was mass confiscation of Jewish wealth along with rampant anti-Semitism, and violence toward the Jewish population escalated. The streets began to fill with angry hordes of people chanting "death to America" and "death to Israel." Many Persian Jews fled to those very countries, bringing what they could with them to start a new life far from the homes they once knew.

Some of the Jews who remained in Iran decided to embrace the revolution and the nation's new rule, and some five thousand of them even took part in welcoming Ayatollah Khomeini as Supreme Leader of the country after he returned from his exile in Paris on February 1, 1979.

The Jewish welcome-committee led by then-Chief Rabbi Yedidia Shofet carried banners in support of the ayatollah and chanted "Jews and Muslims are brothers." It was a sign of allegiance and hope. The hope and exuberance didn't end up lasting very long, however, and Mr. Habib Elghanian—the official head of the Jewish community of Iran—was publicly executed later that year after being accused of espionage for the Zionist regime.

A Trip Unlike Any Other

My flight is half-empty, and I'm fiddling with the carefully folded black hijab hidden in my purse. My headphones blare the tunes of Israeli singer Ehud Banai; I am holding on to the comfort of home until the very last minute. As the plane descends, there is a rush for the bathrooms, women hurrying to put on their head-coverings before reaching Imam Khomeini Airport and the regime's ever-watchful eye. I join them, folding and pinning the fabric as I've practiced in front of the *YouTube* tutorial, and when I meet my own gaze, I do a double take at the woman in the bathroom mirror, immediately more humbled by the heavy cloth and the heaviness its meaning holds.

As I am in Iran officially as a journalist, I am appointed a driver and a translator, both employed by the Ministry of Culture and Islamic Guidance. It's not a voluntary service, but a mandatory one, and these young men are to stay by my side throughout my twenty-one-day stay.

I am picked up at my hotel each morning and dropped off at my door each night, and at the end of each day there is a debriefing at the ministry where we are taken aside and spoken to separately, to make sure our stories match up and are kept straight. Because we spend all hours of the day together, my translator Reza and I end up forming a bond, and to this day I'm unsure if it happens because or despite of the roles we are there to play. We talk about our lives, the commonalities and disparities of our experiences, and we structure our days according to our scheduled prayers.

I'm there to meet with the Jewish community and, as with anything in the Islamic Republic, there is a costly and time-consuming process to get there. Managing to get ahold of the necessary permits to access the Jewish world proves challenging. Tehran is the Jewish center of the country, housing a deeply traditional and religious community with its own schools, restaurants, and religious institutions, and a Jewish Parliamentarian chosen to represent the group's interests in the Iranian *Majlis*. The Jewish minority, now consisting of approximately fifteen thousand individuals with organized communities in Tehran, Esfahan, and Shiraz, is a protected group according to the constitution of the Islamic Republic of Iran, alongside Christian and Zoroastrian Iranians. The Thirteenth Article of the constitution states that Jews "within the limits of the law, are free to perform their religious rites and ceremonies, and to act according to their own canon in matters of personal affairs and religious education."

The limits of the law the constitutional text speaks of is a larger issue than the humble passage may let on, as it applies to the Sharia law that has ruled the country since 1979. Despite being a recognized minority, Iranian Jews are still ruled by Islamic law, and if broken, the consequences are as permanent as they are dire.

The Islamic regime goes to great lengths to either minimize or completely deny the atrocities of World War II. From former president Ali Rafsanjani's statement in 1998 that the Holocaust was "Zionist propaganda" to Mahmoud Ahmadinejad claiming that the Europeans "created a myth in the name of the Holocaust and valued that higher than God, religion, and the prophets," to the current Supreme Leader Sayyid Ali Khamenei repeatedly referring to the Holocaust as a "Jewish myth"—post-revolution Iran has crossed a line when it comes to the Holocaust. One of the most famous and outrageous examples of the Islamic Republic's derision of Holocaust memory is its yearly Holocaust cartoon-contest, where artists denying or mocking the Holocaust are rewarded with cash prizes and gold.

An interesting point in all this is that while senior Iranian officials are denying the Holocaust, the government is hiding the truth from the Iranian public about Iran's own history during World War II. Iran was targeted by Nazi Germany for resources and was invaded by Allied forces. The Iranian government accepted over twenty thousand Polish refugees and a thousand Jewish children, saving them from persecution and death. This is, of course, something that the older generation still remembers, but as with many things that happened before the Islamic Revolution, it remains a taboo subject.

Reza and I transgress some of those taboos on one of my days off, when I ask him to take me around Tehran to get a feel for the city. Just outside my hotel on Ferdowsi Street, workers are preparing for Revolution Day, hanging decorations and meticulously gluing giant strips of photo paper, piece by piece, to create a huge, if cheap, mosaic of the ayatollah as he returns from exile in Paris. Below the image is a sentence in Farsi. I ask Reza what it says.

"Iran—victims never again."

Soon after, Reza takes me to the cemetery to see the graves of the Jewish martyrs, those who volunteered for the Iran-Iraq war thirty-six years ago to prove their allegiance to the land. It's a forty-five-minute ride through thick Tehran traffic, and Reza uses the time as he always does, asking radically personal questions while leering at me unsubtly. This time, his focus is on my connection to Israel and Israel's relationship to Iran, and he wants to know if the conflict between them influences how I view his country. Unwilling to answer, I turn it back on him and ask how he can hate Israel when he claimed to have taken such liking to the Jews?

He answers, "I don't hate Israel, and though I know it's hard to understand from the outside there is a difference between hate and hate. Annika, to tell you the truth, I would love for Iran and Israel to work together and make America irrelevant in the Middle East. Together we would put them out of business. I don't hate Israel. I hate America. Anti-Zionism is a slogan here, but anti-Americanism is in our blood."

We're just a few years apart, Reza and I, and in a different world we could have been close friends rather than the watched and the watcher. It is fascinating to me, how invested he is in the idea of the regime and the revolution. Despite his promises of friendship and assurances that neither Judaism nor Israel is the preferred enemy of his homeland, I am no stranger to the realities he fails to mention. From the Supreme leader's inflammatory anti-Semitic tweets to the now-infamous Holocaust cartoon competition, there is plenty of proof of the things my handler chooses not to acknowledge. Reza is protective of the revolution and of the regime that holds him captive, going as far as aiding and abetting their crimes. He prefers the captivity they offer to the freedom of the enemy, any day and any time.

I ask him about the giant poster outside my hotel, about the message on it and what it means to him, and before he answers, he lights a cigarette and offers it to me, in a rare moment of intimate familiarity.

"It says it all, no? We got screwed, over and over, and it had horrible consequences. Everyone I know was affected by that the Iran-Iraq war in some way, and that's true for everyone here. We were suckers, Annika. We won't be suckers again—that's what it means, I guess."

Despite knowing better, I try to push him on this point. On a basic human level, he wants the things I want—that much I assume—and despite the flaws of the West, I would think there is a longing for the freedoms and possibilities we enjoy. Why is he standing by this evil regime on the grounds of an inherited hatred, and how does that trump the human need to determine the course of one's own life?

"I want this country to be freer, of course, and the tension here does get to me. But I love Iran, and when push comes to shove, I am Iranian. When I meet the outside world, that is only affirmed; that feeling only gets stronger. I want to see Iran vindicated, and it will be. Once we have our pride and strength back, freedom will come, and things will get better," he says.

There is something slightly admirable about the Iranian people's patience for a better day that keeps eluding them, and the national temperament was tested throughout the Iran-Iraq war. In September of 1980 Saddam Hussein's forces invaded Iran, igniting a brutal eight-year war between the two countries. Why Saddam chose to attack Iran is an issue still under dispute. Some say sheer opportunism drove him to attack a weakened Iran in a gambit to strengthen his position in the region. Others maintain that both during and after the Islamic Revolution, Iran had attempted to coordinate a Shia uprising in Sunni Iraq and that Hussein had no choice but to clamp down on what he perceived as a planned Iranian coup. The Iraqi onslaught and the ensuing war took over one million Iranian lives and injured almost as many, devastating the population and leaving a shocked, grief-stricken generation in its wake.

Nowhere is that grief more palpable than at the Blood Fountain. Despite its dramatic name, the water flowing from it now is clear as day. It was built during the Iran-Iraq war as a dedication to the martyrs in the Behesht-e Zahra graveyard in Tehran. Running several stories tall, the fountain used to flow with red, thick water, in memory of the fallen. After the "blood" garnered too much international attention, the government stopped coloring the water, but the fountain remains a permanent piece of marble propaganda. Reminders of the war, the glorification of martyrdom—they are everywhere I look in Tehran. Each street is named for a martyr, featuring plaques with faces and names in remembrance of those lost, and the murals by the side of each major road depict anti-American slogans and imagery decrying the Western world they believe sold them out.

It's an open wound, and the regime makes every effort to keep it open, using it to counteract revolutionary sentiment and prove to their citizens that they stand alone in a world out to get them. And it works. Unlike anti-Israel sentiment, a mere appendage of the hatred against the US, the disdain for America is widespread and palpable. It is found among Iranians of all ages and grounded in a deep sense of history and of being an underdog. Reza is visibly moved, and as we stand there together watching the water, I start saying something but stop at the inhale. Reza picks up where I left off, saying, "You are a Jew, so you have something in the history of your people that changed everything, and you didn't live through it, but it influences how you think and who you are. I have that, too. It changes everything, Annika, and it's not that we can't forget—it's that we don't want to."

Reza is a thirty-three-year-old man who lives every day under the oppressive totalitarian regime of Iran, and despite what I could only assume to be his natural longing for freedom and fairness, he is willing to set all that aside to right what he sees as a historical wrong. As many other nations, Iran fought and lost a long war, but as Reza expresses with no small amount of anger, they felt they had been deprived their right and ability to win or lose on their own terms. This has turned into an obsession and almost a psychological disorder, but unfortunately the regime does not act with madness but rather with cruel deliberation in using and abusing their people in the name of martyrdom and Iranian redemption.

The fact that Reza, a man employed by the regime and who depends on it for his life and livelihood, would openly acknowledge the Holocaust in front of a Western, Jewish, female journalist, says something about how sincere his hurt is and how open the wounds of the Iran-Iraq war still are. The conversation brings us closer and creates a crack in whatever wall we both had put up, but we're both too well-trained not to remain wary.

Because of the stance of their regime, the Jewish community of Iran has had to create an identity that does not relate to the Holocaust at all, making it a rare exception in the world. Not only do the Iranian Jews not have a living tradition of Holocaust remembrance, but they are also subjected to the humiliating Holocaust denial perpetrated by their government, something that doubtlessly rubs salt in a wound.

What I personally found interesting during my time in Iran was the aggressive Holocaust denial and mockery that the Islamic Regime engages in. The Islamic Republic obviously understands how central the Holocaust is to the Jewish people, and it is for that very reason that it mocks and denies it. If the Islamic Republic truly believed that the Holocaust never happened, it would not put this much energy into using it to provoke and hurt the Jewish world and, more importantly, the State of Israel.

I end up meeting with someone who often and publicly defends the regime's inflammatory statements on Israel and the Holocaust. I meet Dr. Siamak More Sedegh at the Sapir Jewish hospital in Tehran, of which he is the director. In addition to practicing medicine, Sedegh is the sole Jewish member of the Iranian parliament. Only Jews are allowed to vote for him.

A man of significant stature, Sedegh emphasizes his words by leaning forward, pushing the edge of his desk ever so slightly toward me with each sentence. During his thirteen years as MP he has gained a reputation for strong opinions, especially on matters concerning Israel, and the day I sit down with him is no exception. He proceeds to instruct me, "The radical Zionism that Netanyahu stands for is just as bad as Nazism, and he needs Hamas to stay in power just as they need him. I want Iran to be allied with Israel, but that cannot happen until there is a Palestinian state, and I don't see that happening until there is a change in the Knesset and in the Israeli leadership."

Watching the pillar of ash on Sedegh's cigarette magically stay put as he gestures, I fumble for a diplomatic response. His amused smile signals that he understands my predicament. His disdain for Netanyahu seems real—as real as anything gets in a system largely based on placating—but from the way he blurts out each line, it's obvious that he speaks from a well-rehearsed script and from intimate knowledge of his place.

I ask him to explain how the regime's—and specifically former president Mahmoud Ahmadinejad's—denial of the Holocaust affects the Jews of Iran. He shrugs, "All the politicians do it. Ahmadinejad, Bibi [Netanyahu]—all of them. They may come out and give speeches to the hardliners among their constituency, but in reality, they govern with much more moderation; and we Jews live within a protected framework. I spoke to Ahmadinejad after his speech at the UN, and I said, bluntly, that denying the Holocaust is denying the sun. And there is no denying the sun."

The "protected framework" is that of the Iranian constitution, specifically Article 13, which states that "Zoroastrian, Jewish, and Christian Iranians are the only recognized religious minorities, who, within the limits of the law, are free to perform their religious rites and ceremonies, and to act according to their own canon in matters of personal affairs and religious education." The central phrase here is "within the limits of the law," the law in question being Sharia.

When I ask what the biggest challenges are for Jews within the Islamic Republic, Sedegh begins by stating, "we are Iranian first," and then adds that the approximately ten thousand Jews of Iran are flourishing, despite some "legal issues" that still require "solving"—such as the law dictating that any member of a non-Muslim family who converts to Islam inherits all his parents' assets. This law has impoverished many Jewish families.

After just under an hour, Dr. Sedegh gets up, showing me that our time is up. Before I leave, I get a short tour around the hospital, complete with a pit stop for chai and sweet pistachio cookies. I chat with everyone I meet, telling each of them the same story of who I am, how I got here, and what my impressions are of Iran. When I tell them I love it here, I'm not lying.

I oddly feel at home here, but it makes sense, given how similar the Persian and Jewish cultures are. It's not uncomplicated, falling in love with a country while despising its regime, but little by little I learn how to hear the double-talk and at least try to decipher what is said and what truths rest in the many meaningful silences this complicated people relies on.

After filling out all the necessary paperwork and vetting, I'm taken to the Jewish community center in Tehran, situated on the third floor in a modern stone building on an unassuming corner in North Tehran. This area is home to most of the city's seven thousand Jews. I see Hebrew writing on the walls, and an old man is making chai in a quiet kitchenette. When I greet him with *shalom aleichem*, he stares at me blankly and then quickly turns his back. My ever-present interpreter Ezra shrugs and points to the room at the end of the corridor where a man in a bright blue suit is talking on the phone in smooth and rapid Farsi.

"Recite the Shema prayer."

Yoram Haroonian, the head of the Jewish community, is eyeing the Swedish identity card I just handed him.

"Should I call you Annika or Channa?" Yoram asks. I now smile.

Yoram's office is beautifully ornate. A large conference table sits in the center of the room; at its head are two Iranian flags and a golden frame holding painted images of Moses and the aging former ayatollah. It is a poignant symbol of Jewish life in Iran and the constant struggle between tradition and regime, and as Mr. Haroonian tells me, indeed, the life of the Jewish people in Persia is unlike any other across the Jewish world: "The Jews of Iran are loyal to the regime, and we were actually the first to volunteer for the war against Iraq. Jewish and Muslim traditions have mixed, in some ways, where Passover mimics the Persian holiday of Nowruz and the traditions of modesty are in accordance with the Muslim tradition, perhaps even more than Jewish *tzniut*. We are Iranian Jews, and that means Iranian first, and we are loyal first and foremost to this country while remaining Torah-true."

The words flow from his mouth with such fluency that I can't help but feel they are not only far too deliberate, but oddly well-rehearsed.

He speaks of loyalties, and I can see why he does, my having brought a member of the regime into his somewhat protected space. Jewish life here comes with carefully constructed rules and understandings, and one of the basic tenets involves separation from Zionism and the Jewish state. Outbursts of loyalty are expected, be that in the form of volunteering for a war or sharing an enemy, and that aspect of their reality is something I, as a European Jew, can relate to and fully understand. Beyond that, the Jewish community lives with a constant level of suspicion toward outsiders and insiders alike, always fearing treachery and infiltration. Much like in the former Soviet Union, people are trying to weed out informants, unsure how to tell friend from foe. In short, there are no real answers, only truths unspoken, and I realize that for this man, there may be a hefty price attached to every uttered word and every answered question.

I ask him about Israel, even though I know whatever answer I get will be measured and made to fit. But I want to know what the Jewish State means to Iranian Jews and if the ban on travel has been lifted, as it was reported back in 2013.

He answers, "We are free to visit, of course, and we can even move if we want to, but we have our lives and history here. This is the second oldest Jewish community in the world, and we are proud to be here, and very proud of this country."

Before I leave, Yoram asks me to join him at his synagogue for Shabbat services the next day and for dinner in his nearby home to meet more members of the community. I readily accept and express my profuse gratitude, as I have been taught is the custom here. Yoram makes a point of inviting my translator as well—as if he is pretending that this man's presence is optional, and not a symbol of the chains he cannot break.

The streets outside the building are frantic, and in the absence of crosswalks, people run with little regard for personal safety between the endless rows of boxy Peugeots.

I find the sprint difficult. Managing the cloth of my floor-length dress while keeping my hijab from slipping is difficult enough without engaging in what can only be described as a smog-filled game of Tehran Tetris. Ezra tells me the smog is due to the "embargo-tires" on all the cars; low quality products imported from China are prone to catching fire and emitting a constant trail of fumes which loom over the city like a pungent blanket. But it isn't just the melting tires or thick brownish smog that hits me. The air is filled with tension that takes just as big a toll as anything visible to the naked eye. It's tiring just walking back to my hotel, and I am overwhelmed both by the city's sounds and smells and by the absurdity of the entire situation.

As the country is preparing for revolution day, celebrating thirty-seven years of Islamic rule, the streets are filled with more than their usual dose of anti-Israel and anti-America propaganda. Walking among all this, as a Zionist Jew so far from home, is an otherworldly and deeply humbling experience. I see a couple cross the street in front of me, and the man is trying to shield his girlfriend from the traffic while quite obviously fighting the urge to grab her hand, and I am struck by how freedom is not just the rights and laws on a document, but the impulses and joys I so often take for granted. A stolen kiss on the way home from a date, a youthful prank or a moment of mischief—those things are outlawed in this land, and with it much of what makes up life itself. So much of life is lived in the unknown and the spontaneous, but there are no unknowns here, only the deafening silence of well-organized certainty.

"Channa!"

An older black-haired woman is waving at me from behind the *mechitze* (dividing partition at synagogue), urging me to come sit down. As I approach, she introduces herself as Yoram's mother, and within minutes I am greeting all the women in what I gather is the honor-row, hosting elegant women of some seniority.

The century-old Abrishami Synagogue is located on Palestine Street in North Tehran, in a beautiful stone building that also houses a fine kosher restaurant, a *mikvah* (ritual bath) and the busy Tehran Yeshiva. Every day there are two *minyanim* here, and on Shabbat the synagogue welcomes around 250 people, filling the synagogue with the same warmth and airlessness that I know from my temple back home. And it is like home, to a surprising degree, down to the same tunes and characters and faces. The nosy women who immediately ascertain my marital status, the off-key men doing harmonies on the familiar liturgy, and the beautiful children running wild in the pews much to their hushing parents' chagrin.

Life behind the *mechitze* offers some much-wanted and rarely found protection from the eyes and ears of the regime—it is there the women and I reach words beyond a whisper, and before the Lecha Dodi prayer, I feel a hand on my arm, grasping desperately for my attention.

"Pray for us, will you, please."

Her words are sad and real and stark, and they break the fourth wall put up by her masters. I nod but fail to answer; I see a glimpse of her life but fail to fully understand. I know there is nothing I can do but say a prayer and tell her story.

After services, Ezra ushers me out, and as the group of diners gather and grow, we slowly make our way to the Haroonian family home for Shabbat dinner. I'm walking alongside the women, and the natural physical distance between the sexes offers a rare opportunity to speak without constraints. I ask the women in broken Hebrew if they are truly allowed to visit Israel or even make Aliyah as I had previously been told?

"We are allowed by law now," the mother says, "but when you leave the country you have to put up collateral, often everything you own, and usually there is only one visa per family offered at one time. So, we can visit, if we do it discretely, but rarely someone leaves. The price would be too high for the rest of us."

Another woman in the group tells me that Iran has the highest number of *agunot*, or chained women, in the world. I am shocked at this notion, as it speaks to a deep desperation, a husband leaving his wife and family behind to flee the life in Iran.

The Haroonian home is warm and colorful, overflowing with guests wanting to eye the Swedish Jewess who has traveled so far to be in their midst. The grandfather pulls out a bottle of wine, something allowed for Jews under the religious exemption from the general ban on alcohol, and he makes *Kiddush* as my Muslim interpreter looks at me and smiles, as if unsure what to do. The mood is surprisingly relaxed, and the women all want to compare notes on Ashkenazi vs Sephardi food as we are served overflowing plates of *ghormeh sabzi* (a beef and bean stew). They ask me about my customs and the world outside, and by the end of dessert, the forbidden subject enters the conversation.

"Have you seen Jerusalem?"

"Have you visited Hebron?"

"Do you have pictures of the Western Wall you could send us after Shabbat?"

It is fascinating to see this 27,000 Jewish community that only has related to Israel through text still feel a longing for the land in such a real and powerful way, and while I answer their questions in vivid detail, I am moved beyond words by the innocence and curiosity of their questions. Despite the regime's policy of Holocaust denial and unabashed anti-Zionism, it has failed to kill the bond between a people and its homeland, even with this much at stake. Religiously, the Iranian Jews have prospered despite living under Sharia law. Ironically, the laws of the Islamic Republic may have contributed to the community's level of observance, as intermarriage is punishable by death, and religion is hailed as the one absolute they can keep to themselves and with each other.

As his wife clears dishes, Yoram presents me with a gift: a large Jewish prayer book in Hebrew and Farsi, with scribbled writing across the back page.

"To our friend Channa Hernroth-Rothstein. May all your prayers be answered, and may you come back to us soon."

I choke up, and neither of us says much; but we understand each other perfectly. As I say my goodbyes, I pray to return safely one day. I pray that if nothing else, that prayer will be heard and answered.

As I leave the Haroonaian family home, it hits me, the overwhelming mix of joy and sadness being in Tehran on Shabbat with my people, a scene so familiar and foreign all at once. To a certain degree, the Jews of Iran enjoy a greater freedom than I, a European Jew, have ever known.

Their synagogues are unguarded, their Jewish identity on proud display, and their religious life lauded and encouraged where mine is de facto outlawed and oppressed. But their freedom exists inside a large and impenetrable prison, their homogenous traditional orthodoxy is only possible in a place where the alternatives are deemed illegal. Most of all, I am hit by their longing for Israel, and how meeting them will forever enhance what Israel means to me.

My connection to Israel is a backbone—it is an integral part of my identity as a Jew. Being in Iran showed me what it would be to live without it. How completely untethered and unsafe I would feel. On my continent, people are fleeing their homes because they are Jewish—their Jewish identity making it unsafe for them to stay. What if there was no Israel to come home to? What if we were left alone, like shards of crystal, dispersed in the Diaspora? How would we act? What would we be? What would we have to do in order to please our masters?

I leave Iran with a heavy heart, knowing I may never return to see the people who became family in an instant, because they always were, and I worry what will come of them once I board that plane. I worry if I caused them harm by even coming. Iran was not what I thought it would be, and the Jewish life not as hellish as I had thought, but in many ways, it was worse and more sinister than I could ever imagine. The Jews of Iran are not persecuted, but they are very far from free. They are living in a gilded cage with freedoms and rights that can be taken away at the behest of their master with neither notice nor reason.

FINLAND

Finland is different.

That much is clear to me almost immediately as I arrive for my first-ever visit to my neighbor in the North. Even though Stockholm and Helsinki are just an hour's flight apart, it has always felt like a separate world to me. Finnish Jews were said to be tougher, taller, and even quieter than their Swedish counterparts, and much like our languages, our lives and history exist side by side with little crossover or similarities.

Strangers and Neighbors

They used to be the same country, Finland and Sweden—for almost six hundred years, until Sweden surrendered Finland to Russia in 1809. Because of the common history, Swedish is still acknowledged as an official language alongside Finnish, and the Finnish legal and social systems are heavily influenced by the Swedish model. Apart from these similarities, Finland is considered an outlier among the Nordic countries, its society being so heavily influenced by Russia, the threatening neighbor to the east. After declaring independence from its Russian masters in 1917, Finland had to fight the Red Army again in World War II, losing precious territory to the Soviets in the process, but despite being forced to sue for peace in the face of an overwhelming Soviet offense, Finland remained sovereign throughout the ordeal. That sovereignty is something no Finn takes for granted, and they work actively to uphold it. At age eighteen, all Finnish men enter army service, and up until the age of sixty they can be called up for reserve duty and training whenever tensions rise around the Baltics. The constant preparedness sets Finland apart from its Nordic neighbors and has created a sort of Russian-Swedish amalgam where toughness and nationalism meet center-liberal values with an inclusive social contract at their core.

It may seem like a simplistic statement, to call this a different kind of place, but it perfectly fits the no-nonsense ways of the Finnish. Their warmth, hidden behind ardent practicality, has made this Nordic country an unexpected haven for Jews since 1809. To understand the life of Finnish Jews today, one must understand Finland's history as well as its relationship to its imposing neighbor.

The military was a way of integration and equality for Jews even before Finland's independence from Russia. Under Tsar Nicholas I, any Jewish boy from age twelve and up was required to enlist in twenty-five years of compulsory military service. This harsh conscription was put in place not merely for military purposes, but in order to assimilate the Jewish population and eventually convert them to Christianity. The Jewish soldiers who resisted these methods of religious intimidation and remained Jews were allowed, after finishing their twenty-five years, to settle anywhere within the Russian empire, and many of the Jews stationed in Finland decided to stay and to settle. The Grand Duchy of Finland was otherwise off-limits to Jews, so the opportunity to advance and gain a level of freedom was instrumental to the Jews and laid the foundation for what is now the Finnish Jewish community.

Even early on, the Finnish Jewish minority enjoyed an unusual level of respect and self-determination, and they shared these rights with other minorities living in the Grand Duchy. Beginning in the 1830s, there was a Jewish prayer room inside the Suomenlinna military base, and Jewish soldiers would share the space with their Muslim counterparts until the first synagogue opened in Helsinki in 1870.

Even though Finland was under Russian rule until 1917, it had some autonomy to make rules that restricted the lives of its Jewish inhabitants, such as where they lived or what types of work they were allowed to do. Jews supported themselves by dealing in second-hand clothes, businesses that eventually became the foundation of Finland's textile industry. In the late nineteenth and early twentieth centuries, several Jewish merchants set up shop in the city's Narynka Market—a cluster of Russian stalls that, after Finnish independence, became a predominantly Jewish market.

In 1909, the Finnish Parliament abolished all restrictions on Jews, but interestingly enough, the Helsinki Jewish community was given a plot of land for a permanent home three years before that, in 1906. The government's voluntary decision to give the Finnish Jews a home was indicative of something in the Finnish mentality and spirit, something that would help both groups as the next Great War was at their door.

Finland fought three major battles during World War II: the Finnish Winter War (1939–40), the Continuation War (41–44), and the Lapland War (44–45). After holding off the Russians in the Winter War, Finland found itself under renewed threat and facing difficult choices—having to choose between German occupation or cooperation with the Germans. They chose the latter, allowing German soldiers onto Finnish territory to fight a common enemy in The Continuation War. Despite fighting side by side, there was never a formal agreement of alliance signed between Finland and Germany, nor did the Finns agree to follow the Nazi dogma of anti-Semitism. Himmler even visited Finland twice in order to make the Finnish government give up their Jews for deportation, but he was sent home, unsuccessful. The approximately three hundred Jews serving in Mannerheim's army did so as equals and were protected from any forms of discrimination and persecution. Three Jewish soldiers serving under Captain Salomon Klass were awarded the Iron Cross for rescuing German soldiers, but all three of them refused to accept the curious honor after war's end.

A Jewish Warrior

One of the three hundred Jewish soldiers in the Finnish army during World War II was Salomon Altschuler. I meet with him in his apartment, just on the outskirts of Helsinki, to talk about his service in the Finnish army and the road that led him there. Salomon was twenty-six when he was first drafted for the Winter War, and he left his home in Vyborg to serve alongside a hundred other Jewish soldiers—their mission being to hold off the Russians, come what may.

Salomon greets us at the door, and even though he moves slowly, using a walker to make his way from the living room, he still has the posture and gravitas of a soldier: straight spine, clear eyes and a firm but brief handshake. Salomon is 104 years old, but he doesn't look a day older than eighty. When I tell him as much, he smiles in a way that tells me he's actually twenty years old at heart. There's a woman in the kitchen, quietly peeling potatoes and preparing fillets of fish, and when I pop my head in to say hello, she tells me she's the daughter, coming here every day to make sure her father gets a proper lunch. It seems as if she has had more than a hand in the upkeep of Salomon's three-bedroom apartment; there's a female touch: perfectly placed throw pillows and a faint smell of Finnish pine soap, hinting at newly scrubbed floors.

Salomon walks up to the big, padded chair in the middle of the living room, and I take a seat in the sofa next to it, almost breathless with an anxious mix of respect and anticipation, very well aware of the fact that I'm lucky to be here hearing this living legend's story. Ariel, one of the heads of the Finnish Jewish community, is with me to assist with translation, but as soon as I start speaking Swedish I can tell by Salomon's reactions that he can understand me perfectly. I start off by thanking him profusely for seeing me, expressing my admiration for all that he has done, and after Ariel needlessly translates my gushing, Salomon answers in Finnish that I should wait until he tells his story to be more honestly impressed.

It's hard to imagine what that would be like, a Jewish soldier fighting alongside the Nazi Germans, and while I try to broach the subject lightly with Salomon, asking how he dealt with the obvious conflict of interest, his answers are clear as day: "I was there as a Finnish patriot, not as a Jew, and I was an equal to anyone in that field."

This, I soon realize, is not to be construed as Salomon hiding his Jewishness or even downgrading it to survive the army; he simply did not feel different or less than anyone else. His confidence is evident in an anecdote he relays to me just as Salomon's daughter walks in to serve us our tea.

Salomon oversaw supplies and materials in the army, and a few months in, he noticed that his fellow Finnish soldiers were not wearing their standard-issue boots and hats. When confronting them, he learned that the Germans—who had severely underestimated the cold and were suffering in the harsh climate—had bought the boots and hats off the Finnish soldiers for a few bottles of cognac.

"I went to the Germans and told them this trade was unacceptable and demanded our things back. One of them asked me what I was, because I did not look Finnish. 'I am a Jew,' I said, 'perhaps this is why I look different.' And the man pulled a gun on me. My command stepped in and made sure everyone knew I was a soldier in his army. Nothing more was said of it."

Salomon and I sit quietly for a moment; he seems to be reminiscing, and I'm honestly not sure quite what to say. Then Salomon smiles, chuckles, and says, "He asked me for the cognac back, you know—the soldier. I told him it had all been drunk and that he should see it as a lesson."

Salomon Altschuler speaks with no small amount of gravitas, and in a way, I am surprised at how very Finnish he is, in wording and delivery. He tells me matter-of-factly that the wars he went through never got in the way of his Jewish observance or his faith, even when the circumstances of the trenches made him break the rules of *kashrut* or the horrors of war tested his religious convictions.

"We prayed in the field and we were Jews in the field, no matter the day or year. I did not serve my country because I am a Jew or despite of it. I was a patriot among patriots, while remaining a proud Jew."

There were two major heartbreaks for Salomon over the course of the six years he spent in active warfare: Finland losing Vyborg—the only place he had ever known as home—to the Russians, and witnessing eight Jews without Finnish citizenship be deported and sent to Nazi death camps. The Altschuler family was, like many others, forced to leave their homes with nothing but the clothes on their backs and relocate to central Finland, where they had to make do with little-to-no rations and a life in wartime hardship. As for the eight Jews who were deported, the decision to do so caused massive protests in Finland, and this apparent attempt to appease the Germans was never repeated.

Salomon had more contact with the German soldiers than most, given that he knew enough German to function as a liaison translator, yet he tells me that he himself neither feared nor hated them. "Perhaps it was because we were equal," he tells me, "there were Jewish officers in our army outranking their non-Jewish soldiers, and that helped us feel assertive and secure."

By the time The Continuation War started, the number of Jewish soldiers had risen from one hundred to three hundred, but they did not necessarily stick together, Salomon says. "My best friends were non-Jews, before the war and after, and in Finland we just don't judge people by religion like others do."

And others I have spoken to echo that, saying that in Finland there is a culture of never speaking about one's faith or cultural heritage, but also a tradition of judging a man by what he does. This explains much of how and why the Jews have found a safe home in Finland and why they have reached every level of society despite having settled so recently in that land. They arrived as soldiers and have served ever since, taking equal responsibility for the country and its many threats and challenges.

Salomon met his wife during the war, and they married in what he describes as the lull before the final battles over Lapland. They didn't speak the same language; she spoke Swedish and he only Finnish and Yiddish, so they learned each other's mother tongue through the letters sent to and from the base. He shows me a picture of them just after the wedding. She is remarkably beautiful, and he is smiling, proudly, wearing his finest dress uniform.

"She was much younger than me, but I didn't know. Not until we were about to marry." Salomon shrugs and smiles. "Not that I'm sorry."

Peace and War

By 1944, Gustaf Emil Mannerheim became president of Finland and signed a peace agreement that awarded the Soviet Union ten percent of the Finnish territory. The agreement meant that Finland ended up in direct conflict with Germany while German troops were still on Finnish soil, and in November of that year, German troops burned down every city in Lapland as they retreated. Not long after, in 1948, twenty-nine Finnish Jews went to Israel to fight in the War of Independence, and during the next two decades, some two hundred more immigrated to the Jewish state.

In the past decades, Finland has had to reckon with some of the more complicated elements of its involvement in the war. It was recently revealed that soldiers from the Finnish army were involved in killing Ukrainian Jews during the Holocaust, prompting a major national probe, and this is just one of many examples of the dual identity that Finland held during those times of turmoil. As previously mentioned, Finland distinguished itself by refusing to deport its Jewish citizens while also working with the Nazis to fight Russia within and outside its borders, and its army, including its numerous Jewish soldiers, fought side by side with Nazi soldiers before turning on them in the Winter War. But Finland has dealt with its complicated history with transparency and openness, making every probe and its results part of public record. Holocaust remembrance and education are a part of the national school curriculum.

The Finns' welcoming attitude toward Jews has survived the test of time, and today, the relatively small community is surprisingly sturdy. In fact, when comparing Diaspora communities' relationships to Israel, the Finnish community stands out. The Finnish Jews are building their return to orthodoxy in part on the connection to Israel, and through that, a very clear and unabashed Zionism is expressed.

Finland and Israel share many similarities, both being small countries with large and powerful neighbors living under an ever-present military threat, resulting in both a strong sense of patriotism and a common responsibility for military service and social preparedness. Beyond the military, they share an ingenuity that has resulted in modern tech-wonders; both Finland and Israel have become start-up nations that are admired and modeled after around the world.

There is a natural brotherhood between the two nations and the Jews of Finland face little to no threat when openly expressing their allegiance to the Jewish State. The open and clear link between the Diaspora and Israel has strengthened the Jewish community of Finland and helped it grow, as Jews now are drawn to Finland—from Israel and elsewhere. Beyond offering a safe environment for Jews, Finland's economy, low crime rates, and world-famous school system has made it a beacon of hope in the Diaspora, and an unexpected one at that.

Finland's Jewish community has been, and is, a deeply traditional one. At fifteen hundred individuals, with the main community in Helsinki and a smaller one in Turku, it is surprisingly vivacious. It is one of the few Jewish communities that has had a small but steady stream of outsiders making a new home within its walls. Since 2010, Yaron Nadbornik has been the head of the Jewish community of Helsinki, and in 2015, he became the youngest person ever to be elected president of a major Jewish community. Yaron runs the community with his twin brother Ariel, and together they have made a point of returning to the traditional ways of Finnish Jewry, focusing on Jewish education and basic community guidelines rooted in orthodoxy. One of their more controversial policies—not allowing uncircumcised boys to enter the Jewish school—was at first met with massive protests, but as Yaron tells me, it later resulted in an uptick in circumcisions among Jewish boys in Helsinki.

According to Yaron, "What we did by demanding more of Jews in this community was to make people think about and relate [to] their Jewishness in a more active way. It's not as if they don't want to be

Jewish or don't want to be observant; they have just been told for so long that little is enough, whereas we're saying that they need to do more. So, they do."

It hasn't been an entirely smooth ride for the Nadbornik brothers, and in the otherwise liberal-leaning Nordic Jewish community. They have been accused of everything from Zionist zealotry to strong-arming congregants into an Orthodox fold—but their methods have also garnered a fair amount of respect and inspired others, such as the younger Jews of Sweden, to ask more of themselves and others. Overall, the Nadbornik leadership has led to a revival for the small congregation, and in 2013, the community hired Simon Livson, its first Finnish-born rabbi—another positive sign for things to come.

When I sit down with Dan Kantor, the man who steered the community for thirty-eight years before the Nadbornik brothers came along, he tells me that the Finnish Jewish community's biggest strength is its members' sense of solidarity. Almost ninety percent of all Finnish Jews are paying members of the community, in comparison to its neighbor Sweden where the same number is around twenty percent, and, according to Dan Kantor, even people who never set foot inside a synagogue or a Jewish school pay the annual fee, because they feel responsible for their fellow Jew. When Mr. Kantor's father grew up, the spoken languages were Yiddish and Swedish, but during his own childhood this would change, and Jewish schools would start teaching Finnish as their first language, marking a change between the older and younger generations.

As for the new and stricter guidelines introduced by Yaron and Ariel, Mr. Kantor isn't necessarily on board but remains supportive of anything that will bring Jews together. "As a community, we're not really that religious and our expressions of Jewish identity aren't always tied to Halacha but rather tradition and culture. But I respect what Yaron is doing, and I'm happy that he has the energy to try."

I'm not entirely convinced that he is indeed happy about it, but what he does agree with the brothers on is their unapologetic view on Israel and the way they have made the connection with the Jewish State an integral part of the community's identity. According to Mr. Kantor, loyalty to Israel has never been an issue for Finnish Jews as it has for other Nordic communities.

In many ways, the Finnish community mirrors others in Europe, with an intermarriage rate in the low ninetieth percentile and struggles with assimilation, but in others it sets itself apart. This is no more visible than when it comes to Israel, where the Finnish state maintains a friendly and positive relationship with its Jewish counterpart. According to Mr. Kantor, this has to do with the similarities between the two countries, being small nations with threatening neighbors and a solid national defense. As for Zionism within the community, the president, Yaron Nadbornik, stated their position clearly and succinctly: "In the Finnish Jewish community, we don't argue about *if* we should support Israel, but rather *how much* we support it."

It's clear that Yaron enjoys the role he has been typecast in by other Nordic Jewish communities as well as his own: as the rebel with a cause, the fire-starting charmer who pushes his agenda come hell or high water. But the rumors of his extremism are highly exaggerated, I realize, when he starts talking passionately about the interreligious work he does in his own community and across Europe. As Yaron describes it, his own and the community's Orthodox baseline make it easier to speak to and work with, among others, the Muslim community, because there is no fear of cross-pollination, just a search for understanding and coexistence. As a representative of his community, Yaron has met with Muslim and Christian leaders around Europe, and he tells me that in many ways there is more understanding between Muslims and Jews than there is between Jews and Christians. Perhaps it's down to the religious similarities, he says, or perhaps it's because Orthodox Jews and religious Muslims both believe they are right and don't expect the consensus that European Christians seem to believe is necessary to live side by side.

Finnish Jews, Choosing to Stay

The size of the Finnish community has fluctuated through the years, from a modest few hundred descendants of Russian cantonists to over a thousand after the fall of the Soviet Union and membership in the European Union. Nowadays, the most common Jewish immigrant is Israeli, choosing Finland for its world-famous education system and lucrative high-tech sector. As a result, half of the children in the Helsinki Jewish School speak Hebrew—another unusual trait for a Jewish community in northern Europe.

Every week, there are well-attended Shabbat services in the Jugend-style synagogue on Malminkatu 26, and the prayers are read from a prayer book with text in both Hebrew and Finnish. The synagogue is stunning, with bright green walls and wooden benches, and above the Aron Hakodesh are deep blue walls, dotted with decorative stars painted onto the ceiling. There are remnants of Finland's dramatic Jewish history everywhere; from the Torah scroll that was rescued by a Jewish soldier in the Crimean War and the crown above the Ark that was taken from an old Swedish warship before it was sunk, to the two menorahs on the sanctuary's front wall with Stars of David hanging from them—each star inscribed with the name of a Jewish soldier who died defending Finland in one of its many battles. The synagogue and its interior are not only a living tribute to Finnish Jewry, but also a tribute to these Jews' position and contribution to that history: shaping it rather than merely being shaped by it.

Salomon Altschuler did both those things, and in many ways, he is a symbol of Finland and its contradictions—the homogenous melting pot above the Arctic Circle. During Salomon's lifetime, the Jewish community has gone through considerable change. Growing up in Vyborg, eighty-five percent of the Jews in Helsinki kept kosher, and all but a few identified as Orthodox. There was no intermarriage, but instead women were brought into Finland from neighboring countries to make a *shidduch* for the local men. Salomon keeps kosher, but at 104 he cannot walk all the way to synagogue for services anymore, relying on his family to make the *seders* for Passover and show up for the High Holidays.

Some of Salomon's friends went to Israel in 1948 to fight, and some remained to make a life there. Salomon himself chose Finland, although some of his children now live in the Jewish state, and he tells me that in hindsight, he is happy about his decision. "Being a Jew in Finland, I have wanted for nothing. I am happy here. I am wanted here. This is home."

Salomon is not alone in feeling this way. The Jews of Finland feel wanted and welcome, and they are comfortable in living side by side with non-Jews as equal citizens. It is not unthinkable that, at least in modern times, this is related to their relatively low level of immigration. There are approximately seventy thousand Muslims in Finland compared to approximately nine hundred thousand in neighboring Sweden, and anti-Semitism is not a factor in the lives of Finnish Jews. Another important factor is the Finnish government's good relationship with Israel, thus not putting the Jewish minority in the position of its Swedish counterpart, which is constantly struggling with accusations of dual loyalties and fear of repercussions in times of military conflict between Israel and its enemies.

The Finnish Jews are not forced to choose between their identities, so they can be Finns and Jews and Zionists all at once, making Finland feel like a home to them rather than a temporary dwelling.

Challenges

It's not all roses, though, and just as its neighbors, the Finnish community has considerable costs for its security, reacting to global developments rather than threats posed from within its borders. Former community head Dan Kantor says he would wear his *kippah* in the street fifteen years ago, but that he would not do it today. This, he says, is not out of a real threat but rather the mood in Europe in the past decade. Finland's membership in the European Union has made the Jewish minority feel less safe, given the free movement between the membership countries and how it has brought global terrorism closer, making a previously remote threat feel tangible and real.

A Difference

Finland is different. When asking the Jews in Finland *why* it is different, they tell me that the community is intensely Zionist, intensely traditional, and intensely Finnish in nature. It reminds me of America, in a way, how minorities are integrated but not assimilated through a culture of dual identity. You are Finnish-Jewish like you are Jewish-American, and in both countries your belonging is judged by your adherence to the social contract and common ideals rather than by your ethnicity. Once upon a time, the Jews came here because they had persevered through the many trials and tests the tsar had put them through, and they were accepted as Finns on merit, having truly earned their spot. That idea, that entrance exam, still seems valid, and the modern Finnish Jew exhibits a confidence that is rarely found in this part of the world.

It seems to me that Finland's Jewish community has cracked some sort of code, where it actively goes against the grain of modern Europe and chooses tradition over trend. The question now is whether those choices will mean survival for Finland's Jews—or simply a more dignified demise.

Rabbi Pinhas Punturello at the Tower of Inquisition

Man at morning prayers at the Bukhari Synagogue in Tashkent

Nisim Amado standing by his father's grave, Istanbul

Avi Chay and Shimon Bitan at their jewelry store in Djerba

The author at the tomb of Esther and Mordechai

Rabbi Aharon Wagner, Irkutsk Synagogue

Salomon Altschuler, Helsinki

Entrance to the Lazama Synagogue, Marrakech

Jewish man in Havana, Cuba

Iranian Jews studying Torah, Tehran

104

Isse Blecher, Stockholm

SIBERIA

It makes sense that in the regional dialect of Ostyak, Siberia means "The End." This vast landscape, spanning from the Ural Mountains to the Pacific Ocean and from the Arctic Ocean all the way to the borders of Kazakhstan, China and Mongolia, has meant the end for many lives throughout history. Ironically, however, it has also meant a new beginning for many Jews.

Siberia is like a country in and of itself, spanning over 5.1 million square miles across much of northern Asia and Eurasia. Before it came under Russian control in the sixteenth and seventeenth centuries, it was home to myriad nomadic peoples: from Enets, Huns, and Turkish Uyghurs to the Mongols and the Khanate of Sibir. The Russian takeover of Siberia started with the arrival of the Cossacks and was followed by Russian military men who were sent up north to settle the land and establish a presence in what would end up being a strategically important Russian oblast.

By the late seventeenth century, Russia had established control of much of Siberia, but what made Russian migration to Siberia go from a trickle to a wave was the construction of the Trans-Siberian Railway in the late nineteenth and early twentieth centuries, which allowed millions of people to relocate and Russia to take advantage of Siberia's vast natural resources.

From the get-go, Siberia was also used as a storage facility for dissidents. Its cold, unforgiving landscape became home to gulags—prisons and work camps for "enemies" of the State. As early as the seventeenth century, the very word "Siberia" was synonymous with hardship and pain, rumors of what went on there traveling across the Russian Empire. Yet to some, Siberia simply became "home."

Coming Home

For me, traveling to Siberia feels almost like a homecoming. Being of partial Russian ancestry, I have always wondered what these edges of the world looked like, and when I finally see it for myself, it's both less and more exotic than I expected.

I get to Irkutsk at 7:00 a.m. Going on just a couple hours of sleep, I decide to hire a driver and travel to see the great Lake Baikal. It's early November and freezing cold, and once fully immersed in a Siberian traffic jam where drivers, including my own, disregard safety, I start to question my decision. We travel for a few hours on long stretches of straight, unmanaged roads patched by snow and ice while listening to upbeat Balkan pop music. It's less scenic than I expected, but as soon as we get to the Baikal, I am glad to have forgone sleep for the breathtaking yet understated beauty of the Siberian seaside.

My driver doesn't speak English, and he laughs at my Russian, which comprises words from my ninth grade tutoring and are solely related to grandmothers standing on balconies and telephone chit-chat. My inability to make myself understood doesn't matter though, because Ilia and I bond quickly over my unintended hilarity, and on the ride back from The Baikal we go on several unscheduled detours.

The first is Ilia's favorite: a hut in the heart of the Siberian forest, painted red many moons ago. Outside the hut there's a huge, stuffed bear, and Ilia points to the door, barely able to contain his excitement. I'm not sure what I expected to see inside, but it wasn't the chained, pacing brown bear that looked up at me as I entered. My shocked reaction seems to please Ilia, as well as the toothless old man who sells tickets to this literal sideshow. For under a dollar, you get to watch this pained animal, once free and majestic, pace back and forth between the trough and the iron bars; and as hard as I try to be respectful of my temporary hosts, I tear up, heartbroken by the undignified scene.

We take our leave and head back to Irkutsk, but with a few hours left before I can check in to my hotel, Ilia offers to show me the city. Without any real means of communication, we enjoy our mid-morning tour, going from Orthodox churches to war memorials, stopping for the occasional Siberian-style shopping spree. I fill thin plastic bags with shawls, matryoshka (nesting) dolls, and Putin-themed coffee mugs. Ilia watches me with amused curiosity as I kneel in dirt, clutching my camera to capture scenes from his reality.

With time to spare, I finally work up the courage to try and explain to Ilia that I want to visit the synagogue in the center of the city. Using my very basic Russian skills and wild assumptions, I point at a map and say "synagogiya," repeatedly, and some thirty minutes later I am dropped off in front of a giant metal menorah.

Hundreds of years before I set foot outside the Irkutsk synagogue, the first Jews arrived in Siberia, most of them from Lithuanian towns captured by the Russians in the Russian-Polish war that spanned between 1632 and 1634.

Seeing the harsh landscape, even as it's clad in modern clothing, it is easy to imagine the hardship the newcomers went through, having to build new lives and entire new communities alongside prisoners, political adversaries to the tsar, and other elements deemed societally unfit.

Siberia has always been synonymous with prisons, forced exile, and labor camps; it was a place you were forced to go and never a home you made by choice. In 1635, as the Tsar Mikhail Romanov fought the Polish Lithuanian Kingdom, a special decree was issued forcing all captured war prisoners—Lithuanians, Germans and Jews—to be forcefully resettled in Siberia. This was not only a practical place to put lawbreakers, but also an effective way to get rid of political opponents and troublemakers.

Once it became known that the enormous territory contained vast natural resources like coal, gas, and precious metals, the Moscow municipality decided to establish large state-owned industries in Siberia to take full advantage of its riches. The imported population proved a convenient and inexpensive workforce, and so these industries were staffed with Jews, political prisoners, and common criminals, creating industrial hubs in cities such as Achinsk, Nerchinsk, and Nizhneudinsk.

As the Jewish population of Siberia grew, it began to establish real communities, and documents from 1813 reveal that a *Chevra Kadisha* (a burial society) had been set up in Tobolsk, the historic capital of Siberia. A few years later, the town had a synagogue, creating a necessary hub to sustain traditional Jewish life. During this time, there was no limitation on Jewish religious expression. Jews were free to study religious texts, exercise their religion, and be openly Jewish in the public sphere. They were, however, forbidden to settle in the border district of Siberia between the area of Russian settlement and that of the natives.

Geographical limitations along with the fact that there were far more Jewish men than women in Siberia, presented a practical problem: how to create marriage-matches and thereby keep the Jewish communities alive. In 1817, inhabitants of Siberia were given official permission to buy—yes, buy—Kalmyk women with the intention of converting and marrying them. The Kalmyk are a Mongolian people residing within Russia. More often than not, the converted women would become much more religiously observant than their husbands, strengthening the core of the Jewish community and becoming an integral part of its survival.

Then and Now

The Irkutsk synagogue stands out. Clad in gorgeous green and yellowish white, it is remarkably devoid of the armed guards and metal detectors that I associate with a Jewish house of prayer.

The 2,000-square-meter building houses a synagogue but also a nursery, computer room, library, youth hall, a large kitchen, and a cafeteria, and when I arrive there it is bustling with High Holiday-activity.

Interestingly, the 140-year-old synagogue burned down in 2004 on the Jewish holiday of Tisha B'Av and was completely restored and reopened in 2009. During the four-year process of restoration, many old treasures were found in the rubble: pillars from the original structure that had been taken down and buried in concrete during the communist era, along with tefillin and prayer books from the early twentieth century. The artifacts revealed not only hidden treasures but many of the struggles endured by Russian Jews—struggles which brought them here to the far ends of the empire.

Emissaries of the North

Aharon and Dorit Wagner arrived as Chabad-Lubavitch emissaries in 2003, and they are the heart and head of the Irkutsk community, managing everything from the preschool to the weekly services. Dorit and Aharon live with their four children three houses down from the synagogue, and a few hours after I arrive in the city, I am already sitting at their table being welcomed as if I were family. Under the Wagner tutelage, the Irkutsk Jewish community has grown in almost every aspect, and the longer I stay, the more it becomes apparent that my idea of Siberian Jews as a dying breed is embarrassingly inaccurate.

"There are five thousand Jews here, according to the latest census, but in truth there are probably three times as many. Wherever I go, I see distinctly Jewish faces, and every week, a new person enters the synagogue, wanting to return."

Dorit Wagner is a refreshingly unsentimental person, and that is a helpful trait for an emissary in Jewish Siberia. Once upon a time, ten percent of the Irkutsk population was Jewish, and even though assimilation, political, and historical forces have decimated the community, there are thousands of Halachic (through ancestral lineage) Jews walking around unaware of their own heritage.

Dorit tells me that, just last year, there were nineteen adult men asking to be circumcised after having discovered their Jewish identity, and that number remains constant in Irkutsk and similar places. What communism once suppressed has awakened in the modern day. Thus, when emissaries like the Wagners arrive and create the infrastructure necessary for Jewish life, people respond and seek being a part of the community.

Those who are aware of who and what they are care deeply; that is evident to anyone visiting Irkutsk. On the Jewish holiday of Simchat Torah alone, there were eighty people in the synagogue celebrating the end of the yearly Torah reading.

Dorit tells me, "On a winter Shabbat last year, it was negative forty-five degrees, and I assumed the services would have to be cancelled, because no human will brave that cold and go outside. I was wrong. The synagogue was packed, because no one wanted to be *the* person to cause the services to be cancelled, everyone wanted to do their bit. That is what this community is all about."

And the loyalty is palpable, something I am made aware of as I attend a community Shabbat dinner at the synagogue on Friday night. The congregants are noticeably annoyed at me for calling their slice of the Jewish world exotic, as the connotation is that it's somehow small and obscure. Before I can even ask questions, they bombard me with facts and figures and comparisons to my own Stockholm community. They maintain that my community is both less active and faces more of a threat from both the non-Jewish community and government than their own. Not only do I grow to agree with them, but I also understand how such loyalty develops in a place with such a difficult history and where there is a struggle and dedication attached to one's survival.

Historically, Siberian Jews were considered religious and traditional, yet they did not engage in daily prayer services or Shabbat observance. While they did go to synagogue on all the major holidays, they kept their shops open on Shabbat, gave their children non-Jewish Russian names, and dressed in a more "generally European" manner rather than traditional Jewish Orthodox garb. This is not to say that they were assimilated; the Siberian Jews were consistently providing their children a Jewish education and took a mutual financial responsibility for keeping Jewish institutions open and active through fundraising in the community. The Siberian Jews were also known for their Zionist leanings, and Siberia is home to a variety of Zionist movements, such as the

Bundists and Po'alei Zion. When the First Congress of the Zionists of Siberia was held in Tomsk in 1903, it was a well-attended event, drawing Jews from the entire region.

Early on in the nineteenth century, Siberian Jews were becoming more settled in their adopted land and more affluent, working as merchants, craftsmen, and furriers. By 1820, in Kainsk, the new Jewish capital of Siberia, Jews made up four-fifths of the total population, and it became an economic and commercial hub in the region. It was also known for its booming fur industry.

As so often in history, Jewish success comes with a set of predictable consequences. Jewish merchants and businessmen were accused of theft and bribery and a variety of other forms of illegal activity, and as a result, there was an official decree in 1820 to forcefully resettle Jewish merchants further east in Siberia.

In an attempt to change the nature of Jewish business, there was another decree issued in 1836 to provide male settlers with thirty acres of land, agricultural equipment, cattle, and food supply for six months as well as a sum of money to cover moving costs, all to incentivize (or rather re-educate) Jews to become farmers in remote Siberian regions.

Thousands of Jewish families accepted this offer, and there would have been plenty more had the tsarist government not decided a year later to stop the policy of resettling Jews in Siberia altogether. The tsar issued a statement that the relocation of Jews to Siberia "would lead to unfair multiplication of Jews who then would spoil the native local population, as Jews are known for their laziness, thefts and briberies, and the lack of faith."

Further restrictions were to follow under the tsarist government, limiting Jewish settlement of workers, convicts, and political dissidents to Yakutsk and Baikal, and—although wives and girls were allowed to join their husbands and fathers as they were forcefully resettled—males under the age of eighteen were forcefully converted to Christianity and made to join the tsar's cantonist schools for future military service.

A New Day

Under Alexander II, the cantonist policy was abolished in 1856, and Jews were finally allowed to live freely within cities, to own land, and to start small private businesses. For the Jews of Siberia in legal and geographical limbo, the new rule of Alexander II meant a change in legal and social status, allowing them to receive their educations in state schools and choose their occupations freely. What's more, the Jews who had served in the Russian army were now free to settle anywhere within the entire Russian empire. These new and more liberal laws resulted in an increase in the Siberian Jewish population and an overall improvement in Jewish life. By 1860, Siberia hosted a yeshiva, a college for Jewish men, and a Jewish cemetery, as well as several synagogues. The growing Jewish population was viewed by their non-Jewish neighbors as being both wealthy and influential.

However, no good thing lasts forever, as Jews throughout history have learned, and in 1881 Alexander II was assassinated. This resulted in the abolishment of most of his liberal-leaning laws concerning Jews. The Siberian authorities, however, could see that the Jewish population had literally and figuratively enriched the region and, in many cases, adopted a "don't ask, don't tell" policy which allowed Jews to often escape orders from St. Petersburg. As a result, the Jewish population of Siberia hit fifty thousand in the early twentieth century.

Between 1918 and 1921, Russia was in the throes of a violent civil war that ended with a galvanization of power around Lenin and the Communist Party. After 1921, Siberia became a part of the Russian Federation, and this meant hard times for a large number of Jews who were accused of treason against the Soviet regime and executed for their supposed crimes. Those who could get away before the expedited sentencing escaped to China, Mongolia, or Palestine, and all of those accused had their properties and belongings confiscated by the state. In some cases, entire communities had their synagogues taken by the state as punishment for supposed collaboration with the enemy.

In the mid-1920s, thirty-two thousand Jews resided in Siberia, and that number doubled in the ten years that followed because of immigration from across the USSR. With the arrival of World War II, so too came another wave of migrants to Siberia, and by the time peace was called, the Jewish population of Siberia had reached a stable seventy thousand.

There is proof of this Jewish history throughout the city. As I walk down the streets, I see several buildings donning Jewish stars. Some of them are prominent mansions standing as historic witnesses to the financial and societal success the Jewish population has had in Irkutsk. Other landmarks are less inspiring: Sovetskaya Street was once home to the Jerusalem cemetery—a burial place for Muslims, Christians, and Jews—but it was demolished during communist times, stone by stone, and a circus was built on top of the bones. It is chilling to see an ornate puppet theatre standing directly on top of what was the Jewish section of the burial site. Given their history here, the Irkutsk Jews have reason to be cynical or even angry, but meeting them, I'm struck by how they are anything but. It seems to me that the Irkutsk Jews are thankful rather than angry, and they embrace the past as a means of moving forward.

The practical aspects of Jewish life are complicated, as is often the case in more remote communities. Kosher meat needs to be purchased in Moscow and brought into the city. As a result, Jews in Irkutsk keep "kosher-style," meaning they do not keep strictly kosher. The most difficult *kashrut* law to keep, Dorit Wagner tells me, is to not mix meat with milk, as dairy is a major staple of Russian food culture. A big part of what the Wagner family does is educate and inspire the community through kosher cooking. Dorit always uses ingredients that can be bought locally and are easy to find.

I ask Aharon and Dorit about anti-Semitism and how Jews are perceived by non-Jews. Their answers are both amusing and surprising: "Jews are respected, even if it stems from a basic idea of anti-Semitism. There have been several people who, just during our time here, have changed their last names to a Jewish-sounding surname, because it is good for business! If there are two doctors to choose from and one is named Abramowic and the other Matvey, they will go to Doctor Abramowic."

The rabbi sees the same ideas about Jews reflected in the people seeking to convert to Judaism. When asked why they wish to convert, some people say they want to become "rich and powerful, like the Jews."

Needless to say, they are not accepted for conversion, but it is an interesting way in which anti-Semitism is expressed in ways other than through violence and persecution.

I ask the Wagners about Putin and how they feel about the highly controversial Russian leader. They say that while he may not be good for everyone, he is certainly good for the Jews: "You have to remember that we Jews have not had many friends in the Russian leadership. From the tsars to the communists, we have been getting the short end of the stick. Putin is the best so far, hands down, and we are experiencing a never-before-seen amount of religious freedom in this country."

Putin the Protector?

Vladimir Putin is said to have a special "Jewish connection," and a story told by Russia's chief rabbi, Berel Lazar, may hold part of the explanation.

"When Putin was a young child, he grew up in a very poor family. His parents were always out at work. He was fortunate that the next-door neighbor was a Hasidic Jewish family, and they always made sure to invite him over," Lazar explained. "They were extremely kind to him, and he realized that not only were they kind to a child who wasn't theirs, not only were they kind to a child that wasn't Jewish, but they were kind to a child in a time and place when it was dangerous to do that. Thirty years later, because of the gratitude he felt for that family, and for the respect he felt for the Jewish people as a whole, as Deputy Mayor of the city of Leningrad, he granted official permission to open the first Jewish school in the city."

In Putin's autobiography, *First Person*, he chronicles many meetings with Jews that have inspired and helped him, including Anatoly Rakhlin, Putin's high-school wrestling coach who he has said was a father figure to him throughout his adolescence, as well as several of his high-level advisors during his political career. The closeness to the Jewish people may be said to have influenced his foreign policy as well.

In 2014, Putin was one of the few political leaders who supported Israel's Operation Protective Edge, stating openly that, "I support Israel's battle that is intended to keep its citizens protected."

A few years prior, at the 2011 Euro-Asian Jewish Congress, Putin said, "Israel is, in fact, a special state to us. It is practically a Russian-speaking country. Israel is one of the few foreign countries that can be called Russian-speaking. It's apparent that more than half of the population speaks Russian."

And in this, he is not wrong. The massive Russian immigration to Israel has shaped the small country in a significant way, and the Russian immigrants have maintained their dual identity, being Jewish-Israeli and Russian in equal measure. A Russian-Israeli alliance therefore makes sense culturally, politically, and militarily, as Putin continues to advance his interests in the Middle East. Given Israel's close relationship to the U.S., the alliance with Russia is a fence to be straddled, but this is something current Prime Minister Benjamin Netanyahu seems more than capable of managing.

Back to the Shul at Irkutsk

The Shabbat service at the Irkutsk synagogue is nothing short of joyous, and I am somewhat astounded by the turnout, given we are at the tail end of the Jewish High Holidays, when most Jews are exhausted and longing for a weekend break. There is a young man reading from the Torah, and the sun comes through the ornate, stained glass windows and hits the *bima* (podium), creating an aura of light around the boy as he hits the high notes. The service is a mix of traditional and modern and is a force propelling this community into the future.

In a way, this could be my own synagogue: children running up and down the pews, women chattering behind the *mechitze* (a screen dividing men and women in orthodox congregations), and the men's voices raising with the melodic flow of prayer. In other ways, it feels completely different. The total lack of security makes it a much more intimate experience than I am used to; here we are part of the community rather than, as is the case in most of Europe, a walled-off entity behind bulletproof glass. Furthermore, the general atmosphere is much less formal than I am used to, from the dress code to the way the rabbi speaks to his congregants. It is all more familiar and close-knit than most other experiences I have had.

The Jews of Irkutsk no longer live in specific neighborhoods or shtetls but are mixed in with society, spread across the city, and they are no longer limited to craftsmanship or peddling. Around the Shabbat table I meet doctors, salesmen, academics, and builders—representative of the wide spectrum of Siberian Jewish life. In fact, several different languages are spoken around the table.

It's a culture and atmosphere I feel at home in, not merely because my distant relatives were Russian, but because there is a familiarity and warm bluntness to the people of this city who have seen and been through more than most of us could even imagine.

The most remarkable experience during my trip to Irkutsk comes on my very last day there. On the morning of my departure, I get up a few hours early and grab a cab to the old Jewish cemetery. It is a cold and sunny morning in Siberia, and as I open the large white gates, decorated with two large Magen Davids, I am completely taken aback by the sight before me.

Rows and rows of headstones, overgrown with branches, tall grass and shrubbery, all frozen both in time and by the unforgiving climate. I get lightheaded as I walk down the unkempt paths between the burial plots, and I realize I have been holding my breath the whole time, walking lightly in the deafening silence of a place that holds so much history and so much pain.

I rummage through my jacket for the pebbles and stones I have brought from home to put here on the tombs of the forgotten, and I take a picture of each headstone, wanting to somehow remember all of their names, curious about where they came from and how they ended up here. I can tell by the dates and years and inscriptions that many of those buried here were cantonists and peddlers; some of the stones have pictures on them, solemn faces looking back at me as I stand there, all alone in the desolate cold.

There is one headstone that completely encapsulates my journey, somehow, not only to Irkutsk but also as a Jew meeting other Jews across the world. It is the headstone of a man born in 1916 who died in 1946. I think he must not have had many easy years throughout his short lifetime. I don't know his story, and I probably never will, but by telling the larger story of Jews here, I can perhaps honor his life and his sacrifice in some small way.

I stay at the old Irkutsk cemetery for hours; my fingers freeze up and cramp as I try to take pictures. Some thirty minutes in, my phone shuts off from the cold. I'm not really prone to sentimentalism, but walking along those endless rows of names, I allow myself to tear up, because the presence of these Jewish souls is completely overwhelming.

Usually, I leave Jewish cemeteries feeling empty and disheartened, but that is not the case today. Rather, I feel amazed by how, under these difficult circumstances, Jewish life here keeps on going and even growing and that people still care enough to fill their *shul* and do their part.

I came to Irkutsk with a fully formed idea of what I would find and what kind of life these Jews were living, but reality on the ground proved me wrong. The legacy of the people whose graves I just visited lives on in Siberia. They did not live in vain, nor did they come here for nothing. It is a comforting thought in a difficult time and an anomaly in a modern Jewish world that often offers little comfort.

In Russia, the Soviet narrative of the Holocaust dies hard, where emphasis was put on the killing of Soviet citizens. Even though the contemporary Russian leadership is attempting to educate its citizens on the Holocaust, the very word *Holocaust* did not exist in the Soviet Union or, later, Russia, but had been replaced by *chelovekonanavistnicheskiy*—literally, human-hating, to describe the Nazi regime and ideology. Considering that seven million Soviet citizens were murdered by the Nazis, 2.5 million of them being Jews, one could make sense of the Soviets viewing Hitler as a hater of all humans, but one should not underestimate the forethought going into the Soviet regime choosing a collectivist view on the genocide rather than the specific, considering the Communist ideology and its goals.

Holocaust remembrance remains a politically charged issue in Russia, despite the overtures from the Russian leadership over the past few years, including participation in Holocaust remembrance ceremonies and public statements on the issue. For the Jews, the Holocaust is an unequivocal historic fact, but for much of the non-Jewish general public, the Soviet narrative still rings true. As shown in a recent interview with NBC News, Vladimir Putin said that the Russians who allegedly interfered with the 2016 U.S. presidential election perhaps are "not even Russians," adding, "Maybe they're Ukrainians, Tatars, Jews, just with Russian citizenship. Even that needs to be checked. Maybe they have dual citizenship. Or maybe a green card. Maybe it was the Americans who paid them for this work. How do you know? I don't know." The statement, while being anti-Semitic, also points to an interesting distinction that can explain the Jews' place in contemporary Russian society. According to Russian Jews that I spoke to, the distinction that Putin is making is not between Jews and Russian citizens, but between Russian Jews and ethnic Russians. This means that the Jews are protected and respected as Russian citizens but that they are not considered ethnically Russian—a distinction that is also made by most Russian Jews themselves. This points to a, however disturbing to some, logical difference in how the two groups relate to the Holocaust differently while living in the same country. The Jews relate to the Holocaust as Jews with Russian citizenship, whereas the ethnic Russians relate to it as Russians.

Russian Jews have found an ally in Putin and his government, and to a certain extent this too applies to their expressions of Zionism. The Russian Jews are at the same time deeply patriotic and clearly aligned with Israel, and given the number of Russians in Israel, having arrived during the post-Soviet Aliyah, many Russian Jews have familial ties to the state and an unencumbered relationship to it. With Putin's political agenda in the Middle East being what it is, there is no telling how long this relationship will remain as uncomplicated as it is now, and should Israel and Russia's interests come to a head, the Jews of Russia would face a very difficult choice, given the strength of Putin's leadership and the consequences of being a minority out of his favor. But for now, as my new Siberian friends tell me, the Jews of Russia are counting their blessings.

SWEDEN

"So, my mother had a stomachache, and she went to the local doctor, right outside the *shtetl*. My mother only spoke Yiddish, so she brought her cousin with her as a translator, since she was the only one we knew who spoke even a few words of Swedish. The doctor asked my mother how long she has had an upset stomach, and my mother says it started at Tisha B'Av. The doctor turned to the cousin who said, 'She has been sick since the destruction of the temple.'

"'Well,' said the doctor, 'then, I think it's a chronic disease.'"

Isse tells the joke in Yiddish, and he's barely able to contain his laughter until the punch line. He's a storyteller, my friend Isidor Blecher, and he knows that in me, he always has a captive audience.

Isse and I met in our synagogue, Adat Jeschurun, and soon became fast friends, sharing many *l'chaim*-filled lunches along the way. At ninety years of age, he carries with him not only an amazing number of off-color Yiddish jokes but a significant portion of Swedish-Jewish history.

Most people think of Sweden as an idyllic, tiny country somewhere up north where everyone is blonde and living large on socialized medicine and state-sponsored feminism, but as always, reality is slightly more complicated. Sweden is a Nordic country, sandwiched between Norway, Denmark, and Finland. It's not only the largest of the Nordic countries, but, with its almost ten million inhabitants, also the most populous. Having enjoyed more than two hundred years of uninterrupted peace, Sweden has been able to focus on establishing the welfare state for which it has become known across the world, mixing socialism and capitalism with progressive social policies such as gay marriage, open borders, and feminism. After being ethnically homogenous and geographically isolated for hundreds of years, Sweden joined the EU and Schengen, a twenty-six-country agreement allowing for free movement and trade, in 1994. Since then, the previously isolated Nordic kingdom has undergone massive changes and, somewhat reluctantly, opened up its gates to the world. In the past few years, Sweden has become infamous for its radically liberal immigration policies and the deleterious effects these have had on its economy, crime stats, and political landscape. In three election cycles, the far-right party, the Sweden Democrats, has gone from a blip on the political radar to becoming the second largest party by running on a strict anti-immigration platform. This political upheaval has created a crisis of identity in Sweden, revealing a schism between the intellectual and political elite championing the progressive agenda and the people who are forced to live with its consequences.

I enter Isse's sprawling five-room apartment on *Chol HaMoed* sukkot, and though we meet here all the time, something about this day is clearly different. I have always felt at home here, perhaps because it reminds me of my grandmother's house: everything in its place, perfectly coordinated down to the smallest detail. Even though Isse lives alone, this place has a female presence. Someone loved this house and made it a home, and her energy fills the space so intensely that it feels as if she's just about to walk through the door and join us.

Dressed up in his best suit, white hair parted perfectly, Isse greets me with barely contained excitement. I am here to listen to his story, all of it. As I sit down to the generous spread of lox, dill potatoes, and clear liquors, I suddenly realize that my friend has been anxiously anticipating this day.

And so, we get right to it.

After spending many years studying in yeshiva, Nehemiah Blecher, Isse's grandfather, left Lithuania and his hometown of Latskeve to seek his fortune in Sweden. Nehemiah had planned to make some money in Sweden, just enough to afford to bring his wife Tamara and their children to America, but history and fate intervened. As murmurs of war came from Russia at the end of the nineteenth century, Tamara packed the family's belongings and joined her husband in Lund, Sweden, in the small Jewish neighborhood known as "Nöden." Although times were tough, Nehemiah was able to build a successful scrap dealership, slowly but surely adapting to life far from home.

A few years before Nehemiah left Lithuania, Aaron Isaac, a seal engraver and haberdasher from Germany, made a similar journey. Isaac arrived in Sweden in 1774 and became the first Jew to settle legally in the country without having to convert to Lutheranism. That was thanks to King Gustav III, who found the Jews to be an intelligent, industrious people and thought that allowing entry to a few Jewish tradesmen would help the crumbling Swedish economy. The Swedish people were not as welcoming. Isaac wrote in his memoirs that he lived in fear of attack for being a Christ-killer and noted that the forced baptism of Jews was common practice. What's more, he and his co-religionists were subjected to the *judereglementet*: a law allowing Jews to settle in only three Swedish cities with the stipulation that they not marry a non-Jew, lure a Lutheran into the Jewish faith, or work outside the guild system.

By the early 1800s, fewer than one thousand Jews lived in Sweden. The country was suffering from a severe recession and, in a tragic reversal of the king's plans for economic recovery, the meager Jewish minority was blamed. Swedes accused Jews of coming to the big cities with their mythical fortunes and driving up prices for everyone else. Jews were condemned for defrauding the Swedish government and destroying the moral fabric of the country. As the recession persisted, Swedes rioted against the small Jewish community of Stockholm. The Jews' place in Sweden was established, but the small Jewish minority persisted, fighting to find its place in a new land while keeping true to old traditions.

Every morning before dawn, Nehemiah Blecher went to the local *shtiebel*, a private home used as a synagogue, to light the furnace in time for the morning prayers. Isse's face lights up when he tells me about how his grandfather was called a *Talmud Chochem* by the entire community, bringing his scholarly knowledge to the shtetl, all the way from the old country.

"You have to understand that the Jewish life we had there, inside the walls of our Jewish village, was more real than any Judaism I have seen in modern times. You see, real Judaism thrives in poverty. Once we get rich, we don't need God anymore—then we can pay cash."

It's hard to imagine growing up like he did, a few hundred Jews from Poland and Lithuania, holed up in a Jewish ghetto no bigger than a single block. They spoke only Yiddish at first, but by the time Isidor was born in 1929, his parents had ventured out a bit and begun to trade with the gentiles. But they never ventured far, as Isse describes it, out of fear of losing their identity. They chose the ghetto, he says, and as much as the Swedes rejected them, they rejected much of what that world had to offer. So, they kept to themselves, and with the help of the town elder, Rabbi Olniansky, felt that they had everything they needed.

"Olniansky did everything. He was our *mohel*, our butcher, our lawyer, our doctor and our rabbi. Through and with him, we survived. That's how it worked back then—we created a closed system, and we chose the Jewish life."

There were meetings with the Swedes, though. Isse and his friends went to a Swedish school and, although he did not have any non-Jewish friends, he got to know Kjell, a young boy who had made a business out of being the *shabbes goy* for the Jewish families in the *shtetl*.

"He was smart, that Kjell kid. He figured out that we couldn't do certain things on Shabbat, and pretty soon he lined up employment with nearly thirty families: lighting furnaces and doing other odd jobs around Nöden. His family accepted us, and even though we didn't socialize, I got the feeling there was some sort of mutual respect."

The respect that the Blecher family received from their gentile neighbors was an exception rather than a rule in early nineteenth-century

Sweden. The Jewish population remained at approximately three thousand until the late 1800s, when pogroms in Eastern Europe brought waves of immigrants to Sweden. While the earlier settlers had been intellectuals and academics, chosen for specific tasks by the king, the new Jewish immigrants were frequently poor, uneducated, and desperate. A divide opened up within the Jewish population between the old and the new—the select and the fleeing.

Many of the new immigrants eked out a meager livelihood as peddlers. And many, such as the Blecher family, lived in small villages in the south of Sweden, where most spoke only Yiddish. These new arrivals and their alien culture once again unnerved the Swedish majority. Whereas the earlier immigrants had been accused of ruining the country with their wealth, the Eastern European Jews were said to be doing the same through their poverty and unwillingness to assimilate. The immigrant issue was raised in the Swedish parliament, where several conservative politicians called for a new, stricter immigration policy that would explicitly protect the Swedish Aryan blood from being dirtied by people with "lesser genetic material." By 1913, they were ultimately successful, and an alien act was established which limited Jewish immigration and called for the deportation of all Polish and Russian Jews that were currently living within Sweden's borders. Ironically, many of the earlier Jewish settlers lobbied against further Jewish immigration as well, fearing that persecution would increase as the unassimilated Jewish population grew.

During this period, Swedish foreign policy also took a dangerous turn. The government began to distance itself from its traditional alliance with France and moved toward Germany, where Bismarck had begun fashioning it into an emerging superpower. Swedes saw Germany as a haven for humanism, academics, and the arts. Critically, it was also the home of Lutheranism, Sweden's state religion. By strengthening German ties, Swedes hoped to establish a potential sanctuary and political alliances should turmoil strike an increasingly troubled Europe.

When turmoil came, in the form of World War I, Swedish public opinion lined up squarely behind the Germans. In fact, Swedish history textbooks written at the end of the war cited the *Dolchstoßlegende* ("stab-in-the-back" myth) as the reason for Germany's loss. This reading of events, in which Germany's defeat and humiliation was blamed largely on unpatriotic Jews, fit naturally into the Swedish storyline about its own troublesome Jewish population. The subtext was clear: If the Jews of Germany had fooled everyone by pretending to integrate only to stab their host country in the back, might not the Jews of Sweden do the same?

The Blechers Persevere

The Blecher family had managed to build a healthy living through and despite the war, and in 1938 they moved to Malmö, where Isse's father was starting his own scrapyard business. Although the family saw the move as a sign of success, there was an underlying worry that leaving the *shtetl* might mean leaving some of their identity behind.

"We always used to say that the Jews in Malmö were becoming goyim. In our shtetl, we rarely even spoke to Swedish people outside of school or the occasional transaction, but in Malmö we would live among them, in mixed neighborhoods."

Their fears were unfounded, it would seem, as Malmö soon would be infused with new Jewish immigrants fleeing Germany just before Kristallnacht. These were learned Jews, deeply religious, and their arrival meant spiritual rejuvenation for the community—even as Jews around the world were standing on the abyss of Europe's impending genocide.

Isse, now a pre-teen, was enjoying his new city and the new faces that came with it. Every Shabbat, a group of boys from synagogue would walk around the city, talking about who they wanted to be and where they wanted to go when they grew up. Sure, the Swedish Jews were careful back then, says Isse, but they were also hopeful about a future beyond the limits of their seaside city.

"We didn't know yet, what was coming, and I was just a boy, happy to finally have friends to play with and a whole big city to explore."

Isse doesn't elaborate on what and how he explored, and it seems to be a very conscious choice. I can only imagine what temptations lurked in the big metropolis of Malmö and how shocking the shift must have felt for the boy from the shtetl. Shocking and alluring, all at once.

But times changed, and they changed quickly; soon the freedom they were all relishing would be under fresh attack.

Troubles Ahead

In the years following the Great War, the socialist workers' movement celebrated many victories in Europe, and Sweden was no exception. The Social Democratic Party, as well as the more radical Marxists, attracted both the masses and the intellectual elite. In 1921, when universal voting rights were established, along with the eight-hour workday, the country welcomed the dawn of a new progressive socialism.

But practical and ideological changes made the Jewish minority into a target once again. The anti-capitalist press often equated the evil capitalist with the Jew. Being good meant being anti-capitalist, and being anti-capitalist meant being anti-Semitic. Between the well-established Lutherans and the rising secular socialists, the Jewish population of Sweden now had enemies on two flanks.

The growing anti-Semitic menace outside Sweden was also now reaching deep into the country. At the international conference in Évian in 1938, Swedish delegate Gösta Engzell expressed concern about the threat that hundreds of thousands of Jewish refugees from Hitler's Germany could become for the Swedish state. Sweden, along with Switzerland—two countries that had long prided themselves on their neutrality—asked the German government to mark the passport of every Jewish citizen so that each could be easily spotted and denied entry. The German government was happy to comply, and on October 5, 1938, all German Jewish passports became invalid. When Jews applied for new passports, each one was marked with a red *J* on the first page.

The waves of anti-Semitism in Europe soon reached the shores of Malmö, and for Isse, the waves hit very close to home: "I realized that the world had changed when the beatings started. Every day at school—every single day—the Swedish boys would round us up and beat us during recess."

I try not to react as Isse tells me this, to just jot down the words and let him speak, but his clear-eyed and calm description of these daily horrors only serves to amplify the pain.

"I got used to the beatings, and I fought back as best I could, but what really got to me was that the teachers knew, they even saw, and accepted this as some sort of valid punishment."

"For what?" I ask Isse, although I know the answer.

"For being a Jew, of course," he says with a shrug and a sigh.

I ask him what his parents did; how they reacted to seeing the bruises and the blood. How did they deal with having their child abused in what should be a house of comfort and learning? Isse tells me that they didn't react, they didn't speak of it, and he never really asked himself why.

"Or no, I'm lying to you. There was this once. A boy had beaten me so bad that I could hardly walk, my shirt was bloodied and my face mangled from the punches. When my father saw me that afternoon, he cried, for the first and last time. He sat next to me at the kitchen table, put his head in his hands and wept."

And then they never spoke of it again.

At the outbreak of World War II, Sweden declared neutrality. But practicality trumped neutrality when it came to the country's relationship with Germany, and between 1939 and 1943, German-Swedish trade thrived. Sweden was Nazi Germany's main supplier of iron ore, ball bearings, and timber. From the Germans, Sweden imported coal, chemical products, and essential ordnance for the Swedish army. Swedish relations with the Nazi regime, however, went far beyond trade. The Swedish railway system was used to transport goods along with German soldiers between Germany and Norway. From 1940 to 1943, these conveyances, commonly known as "German trains," transported 2.1 million soldiers and more than a hundred thousand truckloads of war materiel for the German government.

The Turn of the Tide

In 1942, a ship containing over seven hundred Norwegian Jews was headed for concentration camps, but it capsized off the Swedish coast, leaving few survivors. The event shook the country and stirred debate, as it was the first time the Swedes were confronted with this horrific reality. Paul Levine, director of the Holocaust and Genocide Studies program at Uppsala University, notes that this single episode—involving a mere fraction of the numbers of Jews murdered daily in the death camps of Eastern Europe—compelled Swedes to change their attitude. Here were Nords—Jews, yes, but Nordic citizens—dying right off of Sweden's shores. Before this, Swedish policy had been driven by a mix of anti-Semitism and indifference, and the Swedish borders were closed to Jewish refugees. Suddenly this one event brought about their reopening. By 1943, the Swedish government declared that the country was now willing to take in all Norwegian and Danish Jews.

The outbreak of war had changed everything, yet in a way, nothing at all. For Isse, the beatings continued, and Jewish life was kept private, once again, as not to disturb the gentile neighbors.

"We were keeping our heads down, and even though the shul was packed every Shabbat, we were quieter now, like when you're sitting in a tent, waiting for a storm to pass."

But the storm blazed on, and as Isse describes it, Sweden was so openly pro-Nazi throughout the war that the Swedish Jews got used to seeing their town squares fill up each week with German supporters. What before the war had been a discrete and often hidden alliance between the Swedes and the Germans was now expressed as proud and outright support. The Jewish community was exposed, with little shelter in sight.

"I remember one day, when I was selling peace-flower pins for the soldiers in the Finnish winter war, being a good Nordic citizen, a man came up to me in the street and punched me, three times, right in the face. As I lay there, bleeding from the mouth, an elderly woman walks by and screams at me 'this is why everyone hates you Jews!'"

For the first time I see Isse visibly upset. He seems to get lost in the memory, one hand fidgeting with the strap of his suspenders, the other reaching for his glass.

"You know what the worst part was?" he asks me, as if he just thought of it, pouring another shot of whiskey for the two of us.

"The worst part wasn't the beating, because I was used to that— not a day passed during the war when I wasn't beaten up—but that the woman was screaming at me, even though she must have seen I was the victim. It didn't matter to her that I had been beaten—I was still the culprit, no matter what."

I can see tears in his eyes, and although the writer in me wants to allow the moment to play out, the part of me that loves him wants to save him, make him laugh, take his mind from the sorrows that he lived through. Before I make my choice, Isse makes it for me, raising his glass and smiling.

"As we say in Yiddish: it is hard to be a Jew. L'chaim, my dear."

The "German trains" came to a halt after the battle at Stalingrad in 1943, when it became evident that the tide was turning. Swedish military radio, which had been leased for use by the Germans, was now given over to the Allied forces. Additionally, the Swedish military provided the Allies with all information they had gathered about Nazi plans. Sweden was now, once again, playing for the winning team. It is often said that Sweden's neutrality kept it intact during the war, but in reality, it was the country's willingness to circumvent that neutrality that spared it the fate of its European neighbors.

That same year, the Danish Jews came to Malmö, adding new blood and energy to the community. The Moorish-style synagogue was packed to the rafters during these years, and despite the outright Nazi sympathies held by Sweden, the Jewish community remained almost exclusively traditional and observant, receiving a steady flow of fleeing brethren all the while.

A New Wave of Jewish Immigrants

As the war ended and 425 Danish Holocaust survivors arrived in Malmö with the white buses, Swedish sympathies shifted. Upon seeing the emaciated Jews arrive from death camps, the Swedes embraced them, at least temporarily.

When I ask Isse if it was shocking to him and the other Swedish Jews to see the survivors and be confronted with the atrocities of the war, he surprises me by saying that no, the Jews were not half as shocked as the Swedes.

"The goyim were acting as if this was the first sighting of evil since God was a boy, but we Jews, we weren't that surprised. We knew, we always know, that this is what happens to us. We are hunted down and killed; we are persecuted for who we are, so seeing that hatred and evil take on mass-production was not a great shock to any of us."

Those words send a chill down my spine, for they ring true to me, even today. We expect the worst because we've seen the worst, and none of us have the luxury of shock in the face of atrocities. This was true for my friend, Isse, and this is still true for me.

Isse's reaction to evil was not to engage in sentimental sympathies, but to learn how to fight back. After ending his formal education in the Malmö public school system in the fall of 1947, Isse traveled the six hours by train to Stockholm to train for the *Haganah* (a predecessor of the Israeli Defense Force) alongside Jews from all over Scandinavia. The dream of a Jewish State was not a romantic vision for Isse, but one born of absolute necessity. Even though he feared the impending war, he knew that he and his fellow Scandinavian Jews all had a stake in ensuring Israel's birth.

"It was a shock to see how different the other Jews were, especially the Finns. They were waking up at 5:00 a.m. to march across the grounds in perfect formation while singing Jewish songs at the top of their lungs. They were strong in a way I had never seen Jews be before."

Isse made the mistake of telling his uncle about the plans to go fight in Israel, and soon enough the uncle told his mother that if her boy went, he might never come back to her. That spelled the end of Isse's career as a soldier, and even though he refuses to expand on the issue, it's clear to me that there's a certain shame attached to being one of the few who stayed behind.

"She told me that leaving would be the death of her—so what was I supposed to do? Of course, I regret it now, especially given that all the Swedes who left came back alive, but then again, who knows what my life would have been if I went? Would I have this? Would I have been the same person?"

Sweden had come through the war relatively unscathed. Many Swedes saw themselves as heroes. Stories abounded of the Swedish diplomat Raoul Wallenberg's valiant rescue of thousands of Jews and Count Folke Bernadotte's "white buses" full of liberated concentration-camp victims.

For decades after the war, the country thrived economically, and the Swedish Left carried out various social reforms, creating the welfare state that is still in place today. The new level of Swedish comfort at home included its Jews. The Jewish population settled into a quiet but relatively successful life. With the sudden addition of three thousand Polish Jews fleeing violence in 1968, their numbers rose to fifteen thousand.

Isse and Ingrid

In 1952, as the war slowly started to fade to memory, Isse met Ingrid. He first saw her across the room in a crowded Malmö restaurant. Thinking she was a French actress or model, he imagined that she was merely visiting on her way to some faraway exotic place.

"Ingrid was never a girl, she was always a lady," Isse says to me, trying to describe what first drew him in.

They met for a walk the next day, and one date became many. Before they knew what was even happening, they were already in love. Ingrid, however, was not a French actress on her way through town, but a

Christian girl from a village a few miles away. She wasn't Jewish. And so, their budding romance turned quickly into an impossible dream. As much as it pained him, Isse put a stop to their courtship, explaining to Ingrid that it was unthinkable for him to ever marry outside of his faith. Even though they had said their goodbyes, they kept in contact, exchanging weekly letters for over a year. Ingrid had gone to New York to start over, and Isse focused on building his business, neither of them finding another; both of them still holding on.

In one of her letters, Ingrid tells Isse that she has decided to convert, although he had never asked this of her or even imagined it a possibility. Eighteen months later, Ingrid joined the Jewish people out of will, love, and conviction, having waited for the love of her life for the better part of two years. In 1954, Isse and Ingrid married in the Copenhagen synagogue, accompanied by two families who never thought they would see the day. In their wedding photos, Ingrid is beaming radiantly, while Isse looks perfectly calm and collected.

"I *was* calm," he says as I point this out to him, "I never worried again after that day, because she was there with me, and I felt nothing but peace."

Ingrid died in 2012, and ever since then, Isse honors her. By teaching his housekeeper to cook the dishes she made, just the way she made them. By keeping the house just the way she liked it. By taking care of himself and not giving up, because he knows she would have none of that. Every time we meet, he talks about her: about her blue eyes, her cooking, her *yiddishkeit*, the way she made him feel like a king every time he walked through the door.

"I still keep her wedding dress in my closet. Perfectly pressed, just the way she would have kept it. It's next to the *tzitzit* I wore when we first met. One day I'll take it with me when I go. When I go to see her."

In Ingrid, Isse found his peace, after years of torment and strife. She welcomed Jewish life with love, respect, and enthusiasm. Together they built a business, a home, and togetherness worthy of envy. It's hard to understand in this day and age, but choosing to marry the love of his life—a convert—was a radical choice for the orthodox boy from the shtetl. Although, in time, she came to tolerate Ingrid, Isse's mother never accepted his choice, and being able to withstand that scrutiny, believing he had a right to be happy, was something that Isse says Ingrid brought into his life.

"She had grown up in a Christian home, far from the hardship of the shtetl, and she had never known any of the things my family went through every day. Ingrid had confidence, and joy, and so many other things I never really knew existed, and she gave them all to me. She made me feel like I belonged, that this scrappy Litvak Jew could be accepted into the fancy parlors."

I ask Isse how it felt to go against the grain, against even his own family, to marry Ingrid and choose a life outside of the shtetl, if you will, and he tells me that while he was perhaps not born a fighter, he was made one by life and circumstance: "I have been at war all my life, always fought for survival in one way or another. So that fight was nothing, compared to what I've been through."

In the decades following World War II, Sweden used the fortunes it had amassed through its neutrality to build the modern welfare state it is known for all across the world. Soon, the small Nordic kingdom went from feudal to futuristic, but despite its modern push, old prejudices survived the national overhaul. In the wake of the Holocaust, anti-Semitism hadn't died; it had merely gone to ground. Following the Six-Day War, anti-Semitism returned in raw form. The Swedish press depicted Israel as a power-hungry aggressor, and the left-leaning media used classic anti-Semitic imagery to indict all Jews.

Strange Bedfellows Once More

In 1969, Olof Palme, a charismatic and well-spoken Social Democrat, became Prime Minister. Palme was not only fiercely anti-American and anti-capitalist, he also believed in a Swedish alliance with the Palestine Liberation Organization. He called Yasser Arafat a personal friend and invited him to Sweden on official visits. With Palme as Prime Minister, old stereotypes turned into modern foreign policy, and anti-Semitism found cover in official anti-Zionism. Palme ensured that the PLO received generous Swedish aid, a tradition continuing through today. Sweden gives the Palestinian Authority one hundred million dollars annually.

In 1986, Olof Palme was shot to death in central Stockholm. After the assassination, the prominent Swedish politician Per Gahrton spoke on *Radio Islam* expressing his suspicion that the Mossad was behind the deed. "Individual murders," he noted, "are part of the Zionist strategy." A few decades later, Donald Boström, a prominent Swedish journalist, publicly accused the IDF of harvesting the organs of Palestinian children and selling them for profit. It is worth noting that neither statement was met with public outrage or condemnation.

Every time there's a new headline about Israel or a new attack on our community, Isse calls me, and we lament over the phone. We speak at least once a week, Isse and I, and whatever the initial upset, we always end up debating the fate of Swedish Jewry. One might think that being ninety would slow him down or mellow his mood, but the fact that he has seen so much seems to accomplish the opposite. Isse is angry. Angry and concerned. About the growing anti-Semitism he sees outside his window. The loss of faith in Europe. The slow, but steady decline of tradition.

We all have good reason to be furious. In recent years, Sweden has become synonymous with anti-Semitism, but anyone thinking that this is a new and passing trend would be sorely mistaken. Anti-Semitism preceded the Jews by hundreds of years; before the first Jew settled here, he was already familiar as the unclean and ungodly murderer of Christ.

The popular story concerning the Jews has remained unchanged, even if the tellers of the tale have not. They used to be clergymen and peasants, but today they are politicians and intellectuals with an influence easily rivaling that of their anti-Semitic forbearers. So, when a Swedish journalist wrote in the nation's largest newspaper that IDF soldiers were harvesting organs from Palestinian children, the general public believed him. And even those who didn't quite accept the tale as fact were undoubtedly struck by an ancient familiarity with its general thrust. In what is now the most secular country in the world, it is hard to stir up hatred for the Jewish villain as the killer of God's son. But the imagery of old is easily recycled, and Christ has become the Palestinian child, slaughtered by the chosen people.

Furthermore, recent demographic shifts are making Sweden's population especially receptive to such tales. Between 1948 and 2016, nearly a million individuals were granted asylum in Sweden. As a function of its open-border policy and generous laws regarding familial immigration, the country has seen a drastic change in its basic demographic composition. According to the Swedish national bureau of statistics, more than 260,000 people immigrated to Sweden in 2016, and the four most common countries of origin were Afghanistan, Iraq, Somalia, and Syria. As of 2018, there are an estimated nine hundred thousand Muslims in Sweden, a country with a total population of less than ten million. Sweden's Jewish population, though, still stands at between thirteen and fifteen thousand.

When members of the Muslim community express hatred toward Jews, physically and verbally, it's labeled as an isolated incident fueled by the "Middle East conflict." This is a conflict, moreover, about which Swedish public opinion is thoroughly resolved; a Transatlantic Trends poll from 2012 shows that sixty-eight percent of Swedes have a "very negative" view of Israel. This is the highest negative rating of the Jewish state among the twelve polled countries in the European Union. The strong anti-Israel sentiment has created an almost lawless state for the Jewish minority of Sweden, where crimes against us are too often met with a judicial shrug. In late 2017, for example, three Arab men threw Molotov cocktails into the windows of the Gothenburg synagogue. It was Saturday night, and the Jewish youth club was having its yearly party. It was only by the grace of God that the fire could be put out, and no one died on that cold December evening. The assailants were caught shortly thereafter, and it turned out that all three were newly arrived immigrants from Syria and Palestine—one of them having arrived just six months before the crime. At trial, they were sentenced to two years in prison and deportation, but any sense of relief the Jewish community felt was proven premature. A few months after that, the court of appeals overturned the deportation for the Palestinian man, citing Israel as a reason.

The judge in the case issued a statement saying that since the man committed a crime that "could be perceived as a threat to other Jews," and that Israel "might be interested in the matter," the appeals court ruled that one "cannot safeguard the man's fundamental human rights if he is deported to Palestine."

So apparently, not only are anti-Semitic attacks not being discouraged or punished in Sweden, but they have even become a quick and easy way to be granted asylum.

There are hundreds of examples just like this—attacks on Jewish individuals and institutions, anti-Israel policies, and political attempts to outlaw Jewish rituals, such as circumcision or the import of kosher meat. There is no need to outlaw kosher slaughter, as that law was already passed way back in 1937. As of 2018, Swedish Jewry has few friends to turn to. Jews choose not to wear Jewish symbols, such as stars of David or *yarmulkes*, outside of the synagogue, and any Jewish event is heavily guarded by Swedish police as well as private security measures, making security the community's single biggest expense.

But the threats facing Sweden's Jewry aren't merely from without. In a 2015 *Gallup* study on the least religious countries in the world, Sweden ranked second—losing only to China. According to the Swedish government, only eight percent of all Swedes regularly attend religious services. This, along with the aforementioned political, contemporary, and historical anti-Semitism, has resulted in a high level of assimilation and intermarriage. The community is one in which the majority of Jews identify with Jewish culture rather than Jewish law; Jewish cultural events draw much larger crowds than the regular Shabbat services; and with every generation there are fewer people choosing to keep kosher, circumcise their sons, and make a conscious effort to find a Jewish partner.

Fighting for the Future

There is a silver lining, however, in a young generation of Swedish Jews once again embracing Orthodoxy. This change may be the result of two different agents. Organizations such as the religious Zionist youth group Bnei Akiva work tirelessly to instill in Swedish youth a desire to become active participants in their own faith. And ironically, Jewish practice—Orthodoxy—is quickly becoming a form of youthful rebellion in an otherwise secular and anti-Zionist country. The question, going forward, is whether or not these young Swedish Jews will choose to make Aliyah and build their futures in Israel or if they'll stay and reshape the community. Will they take over its leadership, giving it a new lease on life?

Whatever the future leadership may be, it will have to deal with the larger issue of identity and how to best ensure a Jewish future in an environment that is both increasingly hostile toward its Jewish minority and almost compulsively tied to the past. In Sweden, a large proportion of the community arrived during the years of World War II. Many who did not fled from earlier *pogroms* to Sweden's safer borders. This, of course, shapes the identity of the community, as it is one based on persecution and survival. From 1930 to 1946, tens of thousands of Jews sought refuge in Sweden, and given how small the community was before the 1930s, the arrival of so many refugees would come to shape it for generations to come.

The Holocaust is an inherited trauma, in that it not only hurts those directly impacted by it, but all those who follow in its wake. For communities with a heavy population of refugees and survivors, there is a cloud of persecution and fear, and to a certain extent, the connection to the Holocaust can replace other connections to one's Jewish identity. In Sweden, International Holocaust Remembrance Day is, apart from Yom Kippur, the only day of the year when the synagogues are packed. On that day, the King and Queen of Sweden participate in synagogue services, and many of the national papers run special articles featuring Swedish Jews—a theme rarely highlighted on other days of the year. In Sweden, as in many places around the Diaspora, it is quite rare to see an unequivocal outpouring of support for the Jewish community, but on Holocaust Remembrance Day, that seems to be the case. This creates a subtle but still nearly perverse incentive: to emphasize the Holocaust and grief over dead Jews above the rights and plight of living ones.

Small Jewish communities have to choose where to put their emphasis, what aspects of Jewish life to highlight and invest in, and which are given a back seat. In Sweden, the emphasis has long been put on respecting and highlighting the past, and few things encapsulate this choice as much as the construction of the Bayit, Stockholm's new Jewish community center. As part of the demolition of the old building and the construction of the new, the Orthodox synagogue became homeless, creating a huge schism between the two main parts of the Jewish community—the progressives who wanted to build a cultural center, and the religious crowd who believed the center of the community should be their house of prayer. It may seem like a small war, but it has had huge casualties, as the lively Orthodox synagogue has weakened in homelessness—along with its core group—and has yet to be offered a new home within the walls of the luxurious new building. For an American or Israeli Jew, the importance of a Diaspora synagogue may be hard to understand. In countries like Sweden, where Jewish life is limited and at times even perilous, our synagogues are the places where we can truly be ourselves, openly Jewish, meeting our friends and family and catching up on gossip between the pews. We don't have the luxury of variety, of Jewish social clubs or after-school activities. Our synagogues are where we express, build, and maintain our Jewishness, and when that is taken away, there is little there to replace it. So, the schism between the Stockholm progressives and religious really does matter, and it represents a larger question within the Jewish world, of what it takes to sustain a Jewish community long-term. Are culture and memory enough, or does it take religion to ensure Jewish survival for generations to come?

Isse knows what he thinks should be done, and he says that the fight to give his beloved synagogue a new and permanent home is what keeps him going every day. He views the progressive push as a takeover, not a makeover, and for the five years that Adat Jeschurun has been homeless, Isse has taken pride in raising hell with the heads of the community. At least once a week, he demands they prioritize religious observance, and go back to what he knows to be true. As he keeps telling me, his entire life has been a fight, and now the focus of that fight is the preservation of our synagogue and a permanent home for its furniture, once rescued and smuggled from Hamburg on the eve of Kristallnacht. He has had a seat in the front ever since he first got to Stockholm, and Adat Jeschurun is as much of a home to him as this grand apartment. It means much more to him than any house he has ever owned, and he's not ready to watch it go to ruin—neither the shul nor the community it houses.

"People are telling me that times have changed and that I should be flexible, but I don't understand that at all. How is a fifty-year trend more important than three thousand years of tradition? I don't buy it," he says.

Isse and I spend almost six hours in that apartment, finishing off a bottle of wine while rummaging through a century of memories and photographs. It's strange, having known someone for so long without ever having talked in depth with him. Seeing my friend in the light of his experiences adds gravity, color, and dimension to this little giant of a man from the shtetl.

I keep asking Isse if he needs a break, worried that I am tiring him out and taking what little might be left of his ferocious energy. But he assures me he wants to continue, and every time I ask, he plunges head-long into yet another pool of reminiscence, adding jokes, stories, and vivid images of a world I never knew existed.

Like the one about Benny, one of Isse's best friends growing up. One day, the two of them went to the bathhouse to clean up for Shabbat because the *mikvah* was closed, and because of their isolated existence, neither of them had ever seen a bathhouse before.

"When I was done getting ready, Benny hung back, because he needed to use the restroom. Suddenly I hear him screaming bloody murder from the changing rooms, saying the toilet doesn't flush. The idiot had taken a dump in the bidet, thinking it was a fancy toilet for the goyim!"

Isse's entire body shakes with laughter, and I'm not sure if I find the story more funny or heartbreaking. Isse knows, though, that much is evident.

"From that day on he was known as *badkakker*—bath-pooper in Yiddish—no one ever called him Benny again."

When we finally wrap up, well into the pitch-black Swedish afternoon, I ask Isse how he views the future of Swedish Jewry. Does he think that there is hope for us yet? He makes a face, like a kid biting into a lemon, and then answers me in the best way he knows how.

"So this goy falls in love with a Jewish girl, right? She tells him they can never marry, because he's not a Jew, but he loves her so much that he goes through a conversion. The day he dips in the mikvah, she dumps him, saying whatever feelings she had are gone. Heartbroken, he goes to shul and commiserates with the boys. How can I ever find another one like her, he says, how will I find a good Jewish woman to love me? Don't worry, his shul-buddies say. You're Jewish now, so do what all the other Jewish men do, and marry a *shikse*."

I laugh, but the laughter gets stuck in my throat, given that it hits a bit too close to home. But I get what he's saying. With an intermarriage rate in the eightieth percentile and many Jews choosing to opt out of community life and religion, it's hard to imagine us turning the tide and salvaging this community for generations to come. On the other hand, I am one of those who chose to return to Orthodoxy—to community life—and who shares Isse's dream of a living, breathing Swedish Jewry. Not long ago, I was part of the sad statistics, of those lost to assimilation and regret, but now I am part of the others: those who see traditional life as a proud act of resistance. This is how we found each other, my friend Isse and I. We are the bookends of this saga, the past and future of a community at a crossroads.

"Say what you will about the shtetl, but what we had was real. Mothers lighting Shabbat candles, fathers saying Kiddush, kids all gathering in cheder. Now, everyone wants out. To what, I don't know, but people fear tradition, thinking there is some magic happiness out there on the other side of who they really are."

When I leave Isse's apartment, it's not like the end of other interviews. I'll see him again in a few days, for the Simchat Torah celebration, sharing *l'chaim*s, as we like to do. There's still a sense of loss, though, as we say our goodbyes. I haven't lived the life he described to me, yet there is a sense of paradise lost for what I will never get to know. A Swedish

Jewry, wrapped in Orthodoxy, marinated in tradition, fighting back against the oppressors, knowing there was no other way.

All that is lost now, and perhaps that is why I seek out Isse and his contemporaries, collecting stories and memories as best I can. They are the last of their kind, and Isse's sense of urgency tells me that he knows that. He may have more of a past than a future, but he is still fighting for the rest of us because he knows the things that matter. He is fighting for all of us—even knowing he'll most certainly lose.

TURKEY

"The Turkish Rabbinate is Orthodox, the community is conservative, and its Jews are reform." Atay says this to me somewhat apologetically as I open up my prayer-book to make Kiddush, being the only one who knows how, and I feel a sense of embarrassment coming off of him mix in with my own joy of being there partaking in an Istanbul Shabbat. It is the end of my first-ever week in Turkey, and I have been invited to spend Shabbat with Nissim, my warm and loving guide to Jewish Istanbul, along with his large extended family. Their apartment looks modest from the outside, one of many greyscale buildings on a residential street, but once inside, I am met by a gorgeous winter garden and a sample of Nissim's wife's sculptures carefully placed in every room. It's not an ostentatious home, but a warm one, filled with personal artifacts and books spread across every available surface, and in the spacious kitchen a lamb stew is cooking to near perfection under the auspices of sisters and mothers.

I was lucky to find Nissim, through friends of friends and online pleas, as the Jewish community in Turkey is famously difficult to gain access to. Immediate and warm, he shows up at my hotel that first day, and I know within a minute that we will hit it off. Impeccably clad in suit and suspenders, with two silver pens in the breast pocket of his purple shirt, I see hints at the successful fabric salesman he was in another life.

143

Now a semi-retired man-about-town, Nissim offers to have his driver take us around the city for a few days, and I jump at the chance to get to know this colorful character.

An Ancient People in Erdoğan's Turkey

Nissim's openness is heartwarming considering that Turkish Jews have plenty of reason to be both suspicious and scared: the government seizes any opportunity to blame them for its troubles, and attacks on them have become a common occurrence in recent years. Although attacks on Jews and their institutions in Turkey are far from a recent invention—the Neve Shalom Synagogue was famously bombed in 1986 by the Palestinian Abu Nidal terrorist organization, killing twenty-two Jewish worshipers, and again in 1992 by the Turkish Hezbollah; and several car bombs and attempted attacks have taken place in the early 2000s—there has been a clear uptick in anti-Semitism since the 2016 July 15th coup attempt. Some would say that the failed coup d'état, dramatic as it seemed, was the best thing that ever happened to Turkey's strongman Recep Tayyip Erdoğan. On July 15th, 2016, a section of the Turkish military launched an operation to overthrow the government and topple President Erdoğan. Soldiers and tanks took to the streets in several major cities, Turkish fighter jets dropped bombs on their own parliament, and explosions rang out in Ankara and Istanbul. For half a day, it seemed as if the coup would be successful.

But then, everything shifted.

Thousands of people rushed the streets, and, alongside police and loyalist forces, fought back the coup attempt until the two sides reached a standoff on the famous Bosphorus Bridge in Istanbul and the government could declare victory over its enemies. President Erdoğan blamed his former ally Fethullah Gülen, leader of the influential *hizmet* religious movement, for the failed coup, but he was also quick to allude to a possible influence from the country's minorities: Jews, *Alevis*, Armenians, and Christians in the attack on Turkey and its values.

At first glance, this was a close call for Erdoğan, but as I came to understand during my short stay there, Turkey is all about the things we cannot see.

Following the failed coup, President Erdoğan cleaned house. Saying that he needed to rid the country of "terrorists" and societal elements that had been involved in the attempt to overthrow the government, tens of thousands of people were arrested on charges of links to Gülen and his movement. Academics, journalists, military personnel, police officers, civil servants, teachers, and minorities were arrested, fired, and harassed for what was described as "terrorist activity." As of now, the post-coup arrests have surpassed fifty-five thousand, and one hundred thousand people have been fired from their jobs. Little to no evidence was needed in order to be punished by the Erdoğan government, and one woman I spoke to had been detained and had her passport revoked by the government, simply for having attended a university with links to Fethullah Gülen—hers being one of countless stories about extrajudicial punishment against so-called enemies of the state.

Even though President Erdoğan didn't directly blame Jews or Israel for the failed coup against him, thousands of pro-Erdoğan Twitter accounts did exactly that, publicly calling the coup a Jewish conspiracy, and Erdoğan himself has since the coup taken every opportunity to indirectly accuse Israel, Jews, Alevi Muslims, and Kurds for anti-Turkish behavior and attempts at undermining the laws and values of the land.

Despite Erdoğan's attempts to paint them as outsiders, Jews have lived in the Anatolian area since before the Second Temple. First century Romano-Jewish scholar Flavius Josephus writes that Aristotle "met Jewish people with whom he had an exchange of views during his trip across Asia Minor," and for many years it was a safe haven against persecution, preceding and following the Spanish Inquisition. In 1492, Sultan Bayezid II ordered the governors of the provinces of the Ottoman Empire "not to refuse the Jews entry or cause them difficulties, but to receive them cordially," and for over three hundred years following the Spanish inquisition, Jewish life flourished in Turkey, encouraging both spiritual and monetary growth. Historians have suggested that part of what allowed the Ottoman Empire to achieve such extended cultural, political and geographical domination was its openness toward religious freedom, welcoming minorities into its fold. At times when most of Europe persecuted and forcibly converted Jews, Turkey let them live within the empire in an extraordinary example of tolerance.

The open invitation offered by the Ottomans resulted in some of the Jewish people's greatest treasures being created within its borders, from the development of the Tu BiShvat seder in the city of Izmir and the compilation of the Shulchan Aruch, to the poet Shlomo Halevi Alkabes composing "Lecha Dodi"—the song with which both Ashkenazi and Sephardi Jews still welcome Shabbat each week—while living and studying in Adrianople. This was more than survival for the Jews who had fled persecution elsewhere—this was life at its fullest and a golden era that would end up influencing the Jewish world for centuries to come.

Modern Hardship

Today, however, the once almost two hundred thousand-strong Jewish population of the Ottoman Empire has shrunken to between eleven thousand to seventeen thousand out of a total population of seventy million, in part due to the economic situation, and in part due to heavy restrictions on and threats toward Jewish individuals in the region. The Turkish community is ninety-six percent Sephardi and four percent Ashkenazi and are represented by a chief rabbi who is responsible for overseeing the six community rabbis as well as the nineteen active synagogues that are located in four major cities throughout the country. The Jewish infrastructure is there—with houses of prayer, Jewish leadership, kosher eateries, and even political representation—but still, observance is on a steady decline.

Some of those I speak to say that the diminishing number of observant Jews in Turkey is not a recent occurrence but part of a steady flow that started with the rise of Atatürk and the establishment of the Republic.

"The idea of the perfect homogenous Turkish identity and the hatred toward minorities flowered under Atatürk, and we still see the consequences of that today, in ways that actually have very little to do with Islam."

Rabbi Chitrik has struggled for seventeen years to establish a prayer room at the Jewish school and to convince the authorities to allow *kippot* and *tzitzit* on the premises, a concept that sounds mildly absurd to an outsider but makes perfect sense in modern Turkey.

"Finally, I found a legal clause that forbids the suppression of prayer, and since the document hadn't specified that the prayer had to be Muslim, I was able to get a prayer room in the school. The *tzitzit* and *kippot* were accepted after I threatened to file a suit against the government for failing to enforce the law on skirts having to be at least three inches below the knee; they caved so I wouldn't embarrass them in court," Rabbi Chitrik tells me.

Needless to say, most people don't have the stamina to fight as much as Rabbi Chitrik, and assimilation is rampant among Turkish Jews. I see the slow changes reflect on the tombstones of the Ortoköy Jewish cemetery as Nissim and I walk along the graves, where the Hebrew is replaced with French and then, the religious text with the poetic. Three rows down, Nissim's maternal grandfather lies buried, and my newfound friend is visibly moved as he knocks the stone in his hand three times against the tomb before placing it gently over the letters of his ancestor's name.

"He worked himself to death, trying to repay the loan his wife took out to get him out of prison."

Nissim's grandfather suffered under the Turkish "wealth tax" that was instituted in the early 1940s, aimed at Armenians, Jews, Greeks and Levantines. The official reason for the tax was to amass funds for a possible entry into World War II, but in reality, it was a way of throwing Turkey's non-Muslims into financial ruin and despair. Because of his inability to pay the massive Dhimmi-tax, Nissim's grandfather was thrown into a prison camp, and his grandmother borrowed money from Muslim bankers in order to get him out. Once freed, he was forced to work his fingers to the bone for the rest of his life, just to manage the payments, and all the untold stories of this hardship is reflected in Nissim's eyes as he stands at the foot of his grave.

Nissim's is just one of many Turkish stories of life and hardship during the Second World War. Before the outbreak of direct hostilities, the Turkish government issued a decree denying entry visas to Jews trying to escape the Nazi regime. Despite this hardline official stance, individual Turks risked both life and livelihood to try and save Jews from annihilation. One of the most notable examples of this is Selahattin Ülkümen, Turkish consul general in Rhodes during World War II, who was recognized by world Holocaust Remembrance center Yad Vashem as one of the "Righteous among the Nations" for personally saving fifty Jews of the Greek island of Rhodes while risking his own life. This duality, between harsh official policies and heroic personal sacrifice, runs like a red thread throughout the history of Jewish Turkey. The Turkey-first, nationalist ideology that inspired the founding of the Republic led to closed borders that rejected fleeing Jews during World War II but it also can be said to have attributed to the fact that Turkey was one of very few communities in that world that did not fall victim to the Holocaust. As a comparison, almost the entire nearby Jewish community of Greece was annihilated during World War II, making the relative safety that Turkish Jews experienced even more extraordinary.

Conditions have shifted since then, as far as I can tell. I take a picture of Nissim as he stands by his grandfather's grave, but he asks me not to post it on social media.

"The government is already monitoring me, and I don't want to give them an excuse to say that I am some sort of terrorist, speaking ill of Turkey or complaining about our history."

I try really hard not to show the anger I feel at his words: anger at how little has changed since the Dhimmi-laws and the outright persecution, and at how the Jews of this land are still locked in a prison of fear and silence. Feeling that my reaction would somehow be disrespectful or patronizing, I walk next to him in silence, reading each name out loud to myself—making sense of the words as the outside world befuddles me.

We spend over an hour in the cemetery, and before we leave, I pay the mandatory optional fee to the keepers of the keys as they offer up water for my hands and seemingly rehearsed greetings. I'm annoyed, but not at them, really. I just feel stuck in a feeling of frustration over the scenes I keep seeing play out all across the world: of us, the Jews, seeing our heritage become museums and paying our masters for the pleasure. So, I cram some bills into a box in impotent and misdirected anger and, ever wise, Nissim notices my annoyance and suggests we get some food. He knows, as we all do, that there are few problems that a good meal can't solve, so I follow him wherever he suggests, thankful to be cut off from my train of thought.

It's Ramadan, and the pace of the city is sluggish in the unrelenting heat. Nissim and I go to a nearby kosher restaurant, and Nissim shows his ID card at the unmarked door, revealing the word *Musevi* (Jew) in bold black letters. The owners of the otherwise-empty eatery treat us like royalty, and while they speak no Hebrew, they chatter in fluent Ladino, one of the few remnants of a time that was. There is a warm familiarity between Nissim and I, despite the fact that we didn't know each other's names just a few days ago. Regardless of geography, age, or our levels of observance, we are just two Jews sharing a meal, cooked according to the rules of our ancient faith. Right below the restaurant lies a small but ornate synagogue, and as we walk through it, we are approached by the curious keepers of the keys, asking for our names and IDs. This is the case in every Jewish institution in this city: the doors are unmarked but heavily guarded, and usually, getting in takes more than one form of verification.

That feeling is everywhere—the low-level fear and hostility. Turkey is a deeply conservative country shrouded in modern attire. While there may be plenty of scantily clad European tourists on the streets of Istanbul, I am told not to walk alone at night and definitely not to wear my Magen David necklace or tell anyone that I am a Jew. Having already spent time in Iran, I am surprised at how this place feels more menacing, somehow—perhaps because the world is in agreement on what Iran is, whereas Turkey still is able to play the role of country among countries while its leadership does away with basic rights and freedoms. It feels like a dictatorship hiding in plain sight, jailing and killing minorities and journalists while millions of tourists take selfies on the beaches of Antalya. Ever since the 2016 coup, Turkey is under an official state of emergency, and even before that fateful day, it had rejected modernity and democracy and moved toward a place where there is no true rule of law. Erdoğan has now entered his fifteenth year in power, first as prime minister and now as a president with growing constitutional latitude, and after being re-elected in 2018, his grip has tightened further, not least over the many religious and ethnic minorities that already suffer greatly under his command.

Erdoğan has achieved stability, says Turkish Jewish author and historian Rifat Bali when I meet up with him in his downtown office.

"Erdoğan is the best option for the Jews in this election. I mean, what options are there? Anything but Erdoğan would mean chaos, and chaos has never, ever favored the Jews."

Nissim is sitting next to me, and he boldly interjects in disagreement, receiving little but a scoff for his trouble. Mr. Bali assures me that the Jews will not be persecuted under Erdoğan and that, as far as he knows, no Jew has even been arrested. When I ask him about the President's constant and virulent anti-Israel rhetoric, Bali shrugs and says that this is a language that means very little in actual terms in this part of the world: "Turkish Jews live a dual life, where we know not to put Israel on the forefront but keep that private. The Turkish Jews that remain here are well off, they live good lives, and they know how to survive in this environment where very few Turks carry the baggage of rational thought."

And he is not wrong, at least not about the last part. The remaining Turkish Jews have developed excellent survival skills, and very few still carry their Jewish family names but have adapted and changed to accommodate their surroundings. There is still more of a Jewish framework here than in my native Sweden—such as several kosher butcheries, three kosher *mikvaot* and at least three daily *minyanim*—but the power of self-censorship has set in long ago, and fewer and fewer keep kosher, use the *mikvah*, or partake in any other form of observant Jewish life. It is a slow suffocation of the Jewish existence, as opposed to an outright shot to the heart.

There have been shots fired, damaging the relationship between the Turkish state and its Jews, and the Gaza Flotilla incident was certainly one of them. In May of 2010, the Turkish Islamist organization Insani Yardim Vakfi sent six ships to break the naval blockade on Gaza, and when those ships were intercepted by the IDF, violence ensued. Activists on the lead boat, *Mavi Marmara*, attacked the Israeli soldiers with knives, clubs, and weaponry, and in the tumult, seven Israeli soldiers were wounded and ten activists were killed. The relationship between Israel and Turkey completely broke down over the incident and stayed broken until late 2013, when Israel made a formal apology to the Turkey and later paid an undisclosed settlement to the victims' families. Although ensuing investigations showed that the activists on board the *Marmara* were the aggressors, and both Turkish and international courts dismissed the cases brought before them against Israel and the IDF, the events became another reason for the Turkish people to question the Jewish minority's loyalty and for the Jews to keep their heads even further down.

After the official apology, President Erdoğan made a statement acknowledging the normalization of the diplomatic relationship between the two countries, and in 2015 there was an official Hanukkah celebration in central Istanbul, seemingly marking a new era in Israel-Turkish relationships. The thaw was temporary, however, and by the time the ancient Istopol Synagogue, built before the conquest of Constantinople, opened for its first service in sixty-five years, it was met with protests and anti-Semitic graffiti saying, "Terrorist Israel, there is only Allah."

As the 2018 general elections rolled around, Jews were keeping well out of the way of the public debate and focusing on staying off the radar. Recent events, such as the embassy moving to Jerusalem and violent riots in and around Gaza, has raised the threat level and caused discord within the community, as many now feel that they are being targeted based on Israeli and American policy, despite doing their best to slip into the shadows. What Jews know, not only in Turkey, but all across the world, is that while rapprochements may be temporary, hatred of Jews is perennial.

A Long Farewell

Nissim and his family listen to me as I sing the Birkat Hamazon, and afterwards, we retire to the living room with the traditional glass of chai and delicate plates overflowing with fruit. We are in a Jewish bubble now, a place of comfort for all of us, and very little reminds us of the troubling status quo that looms outside those doors. By nightfall the next day, I will be leaving, and the family will stay in a country that for decades has done its best to force them out. I am as impressed by their dignity and tenacity as I am heartsick for their peril, and as a fellow Diaspora Jew with centuries of roots in a land that treats me like a stranger, I fully understand why they feel they have to stay and see this through.

Perhaps Rifat Bali was right: maybe the leadership of Turkey doesn't matter to the Jews, as there are no leaders left who would protect them. To seek the status quo, though, is a fallacy, because Erdoğan will likely not rest on his laurels if he lives to fight another day. Mr. Bali laughed at me when I asked him if Turkish Jews faced a possible expulsion under an even more totalitarian Erdoğan rule, saying that this was typical hyperbole emanating from an ignorant foreign media. But after a week in Istanbul, I see that there are many ways to expel a people, or to simply make them disappear. Nissim's grandfather is proof of that, having been taxed out of house and home and penalized to near-assimilation. Today's Turkish Jews are fading into the woodwork, despite thousands of years of glorious history, and while the Turkish government may claim it is done by choice, it is clear to me that this is done out of heartbreaking necessity.

What I saw in Turkey during that intense week is a community that has started to exchange Jewish life for Jewish memory—polishing artifacts while leaving the daily observances behind. Concessions were made in exchange for acceptance and security, but from what I can see, the Jews of Turkey were given a bum deal, divided and conquered without much of a fight. After all they've lost, the Jews of Turkey are no closer to safety, but they are that much further from themselves.

It has only been a week, but I have grown close with Nissim, happily accepting his fatherly advice and protection; laughing at his dad-jokes as I help him up and down the city's countless hills. As we say goodbye at his door, we make the usual assurances of a swift reunion, adding a sardonic "inshAllah," as a prayer wrapped in a joke. In contemporary Turkey, things change in a day—never knowing who will be let in and who is kept out—and neither of us know for sure that we will be able to make good on that promise.

It's heartbreaking, really, knowing the rich history of this region and what a haven it once was to the Jews, and seeing it now, throwing hundreds of years of tolerance and tradition out the window as it's edging its way to extremism. Jews helped build this empire, and now it seems to be crashing down upon them.

As I'm leaving Istanbul and riding across the Bosphorus Bridge one last time, I am struck by the almost poetic layout of a city on two continents, struggling to keep its keel with one foot in each world. On the surface, Istanbul gained its footing, but then again, this country is all about the things you cannot see.

PALERMO

It's cold in here, colder than outside; the stone walls amplify and multiply the chill and trap it inside of this prison-turned-museum. It looks oddly modern, scaled back and empty, almost like an art gallery, but I know too well that an ancient hatred rests within these walls.

There are etchings on the wall of the Inquisition prison in Palermo, drawings made by the convicted and condemned, transcribed from heart and memory. The Jewish prisoners made images of Israel and of their people, sometimes using phrases from the Bible. I have come to see them for myself, in these lonely, stone-clad chambers.

The building is architecturally simple but humanly unimaginable; my heels make an echoing clacking sound as they hit the cold stone floor. I move with careful, quiet hesitation, from room to heartbreaking room. From time to time I put a camera between myself and these murals of death, just to distance myself from the rush of emotion, making this reality a little bit less real.

It's hard, knowing these images are what the Jewish prisoners of the Inquisition chose as their last message to the world. They carved their hearts into that white stone, and what came out were images of Jerusalem, of our ancestors and our home, simple Hebrew words of prayer to perhaps bring solace before the inevitable outcome. One day, any day, the big bell would ring and they would burn for the sin of being Jewish, so they used whatever time was left to leave a piece of themselves behind in these horrifying rooms. The expulsion, murder, and forced conversion of the Palermo Jews may have taken place over five hundred years ago, but the pain within these walls is eternal, and I find myself looking for a reason to leave, as any tears I shed here are insufficient.

I always declined all invitations to accompany groups to the sites of the Shoah—the Holocaust—I never saw the death camps nor went on the March of the Living while there. I could say that I chose this entirely on principle, but that wouldn't be honest or true. At times, I dislike focusing on the Holocaust as the only marker of Jewish identity—as if it were the alpha and omega of our existence. I fear what it does to our self-image and the strength we, as a people, feel and project. But I also fear these places, deeply and truly; I fear the pain of the memories and the anger I feel when I visit the houses that held us, knowing that these debts can never be paid. So, my visit to the prison of the Inquisition in Palermo wouldn't have happened had I not been there for work as part of a delegation, and the reasons for that are not pious, but merely human and weak. These places hold anxiety; it bounces between the walls, and the scaled-down interior only helps to enhance the horrors that went on here, making it easier to relate to what it would be to sit here, on these cold, stone floors, waiting for the bell to ring to announce your execution.

Shoah museums and monuments are often accompanied by plaques with solemn quotes about remembrance and responsibility, but this place lets the empty spaces speak, and they do, at an almost unbearable volume. There is no guide to tell me how horrible this was or to speak of the lessons learned by history. I hate all that, quite honestly, mostly because neither lessons nor promises mean much as soon as the guests exit the doors of the museum. It's better this way, to be left alone with these spaces and touch these walls on which so many of my Jewish brothers and sisters carved their last thoughts and messages.

The only other person in this three-storied building is Rabbi Pierpaolo Pinhas Punturello, who works here in Palermo as an emissary of Shavei Israel, an Israeli organization that helps connect people to their Jewish heritage. Rabbi Punturello has helped guide me through Jewish

Palermo over the past week, and with his Italian/Israeli background, he serves as the perfect introduction to this ancient Jewish community, coming alive after centuries of death and desolation.

A Brief History

Jews have resided in Sicily since at least the first century CE, many arriving from Jerusalem as part of the early Diaspora, and they have remained on the island—the largest in the Mediterranean—until the 1492 expulsion edict. At one point, there were fifty-one communities here, and Palermo was the heart of Jewish Sicily, home to the largest and most vibrant Jewish community. The Jews of Sicily are often referred to as Sephardim, even if they are not culturally. By the time of the 1492 expulsion, when Spain ordered the expulsion or conversion of all Jews within its domain, Jews represented approximately ten percent of the population in Sicily. Six months later, around half of Sicily's Jews left the island, while the other half converted to Christianity and remained. Many Sicilian Jews fled to the neighboring mainland of Calabria or to Naples, both places offering relative safety until the full force of the Inquisition hit in 1493.

The lion's share of the Sicilian Jewish community fled to the Ottoman Empire, settling mainly in Turkey, Cyprus, and Greece, where they were well-received and offered the opportunity to build congregations, practice their religion, and become prominent members of the larger societies.

The expulsion edict affected at least thirty-five thousand Sicilian Jews, including at least five thousand in Palermo. Some of the Jews who had decided to stay continued to practice their religion in secret, despite having officially converted to Catholicism. These "hidden Jews" are known as *Marranos*, and some of their ancestors are now seeking to return to their Jewish roots. Rabbi Punturello is helping them find their way back.

"It's impossible to say how many Jews or descendants of Jews live here in Palermo now, but what I do know is that there has been a clear uptick in interest from people seeking their Jewish roots. They want to come back, they want to learn about who they are, and I think that fire is at the heart of the Jewish spirit."

Jewish history is ever-present in Palermo, from the street names in the Jewish quarter having Hebrew names and some of the churches showing clear signs of having been converted from synagogues during the Inquisition, to the beautiful ancient *mikvah* (ritual bath) that was recently discovered below the courtyard of Palazzo Marchesi, which in the sixteenth century housed the offices of the Inquisition.

There are twenty-six narrow stone steps leading me straight down to the *mikvah*, and there is only a single source of light down there, making the site twice as alluring and mysterious. As I lean against the wall to touch the icy water, I am struck by the fact that I'm halfway under the Palazzo Square. I can hear the traffic and people walking above my head, unaware of the literal pool of Jewish history that has been unearthed in the middle of their city. Hundreds of years ago, this was a center of Jewish life; this *mikvah* was used by thousands of Jews, and there is something undeniably poetic about it being found at a time when so many Sicilian Jews are finding their Jewish roots long buried.

Because the digging has just begun, literally and figuratively, Jewish life has far from bounced back or been rejuvenated here. There is no regular *minyan*—the ten-man prayer-quorum required for communal Jewish worship—and there are no kosher butchers or restaurants available, forcing anyone who keeps strictly kosher to import kosher meat to the island from larger cities such as Naples or Rome. Jewish-themed tourism has picked up, however, and tour guides offer specific guided tours to the Jewish sites around Palermo, many of them holding their own painful memories of a violent past. The city itself has recognized the value of its Jewish history and taken active steps to rehabilitate not only the community, but also the relationship between Jews and Christians. Five years ago, Hanukkah candles were lit for the first time at Palazzo Steri, a clear olive branch and proof of Palermo's commitment to its Jewish community.

The biggest step toward that end is, by far, the repurposing of an oratory—the St. Mary of Saturday—placed in the old Jewish quarter where the Grand Synagogue of Palermo used to be. This momentous step is the result of an historic agreement between the local Catholic Church and the Palermo's resurgent Jewish community, and in 2017, Palermo's Archbishop, Corrado Lorefice, officially gave the community access to St. Mary of Saturday, allowing the substantial refurbishing efforts to begin.

I accompany Rabbi Punturello and the head of Shavei Israel to the official ceremony where the key to the former church is to be handed over to the Jewish community, taking place at the Palermo municipal archives. The archive houses some of the infamous expulsion documents, displayed throughout the hall in glass cases. Seeing the names and dates meticulously written in aged yellow ledgers sends a shiver down my spine. I am standing in the middle of history, exactly where these crimes took place.

The municipal archives are said to have been modeled after the Grand Synagogue, and it is truly a breathtaking building, with its great columns and wuthering heights, displaying row after row of ancient scripture. Once we get there, the hall is already packed with an almost absurd mix of people; nuns and monks mixing with old men in kippot and hipster youth, overlooking a long table where the archbishop seems to be preparing his speech.

The ceremony itself is moving, but short, and the crowd erupts in enthusiastic applause as the key is handed over from archbishop to rabbi, seemingly undoing a lot of hurt and releasing tensions throughout the great hall. Cake and wine are served afterwards, and we mingle, tentatively at first, slowly finding our ease. I find myself standing next to Angelo, a handsome man in a colorful kippah. We find common ground discussing the many culinary delights for which Sicily is known. We discuss cheeses and sauces and how to make the perfect tiramisu. Angelo has been a part of the Shavei program, bringing back the lost Jews of Palermo, and he tells me that he feels as if he has finally come into his own.

"It's not that my entire life has changed or anything, yet it has, because now I know that I am Jewish, and I have a whole new perspective on life and an alliance with Israel and my people. I'm never alone again, and I am honoring my relatives from so long ago who went through God-knows-what and lost this, and here I am choosing to take it back."

Angelo offers to take me shopping after Shabbat, saying he will help me find things from the local kosher list that the rabbi has put together, and we set up a meeting for Saturday night. Not a lot of people here keep kosher, and those who do must go to great lengths to do so. Angelo does his best to keep kosher, but he is far from strict. Rather, he does what he can when he can and accepts the situation for what it is. He says he feels gratitude for having come this far. When I ask him when he feels the most Jewish and connected to his Jewishness, he immediately tells me "in Israel" and goes on to say that since his return to his roots, he has visited the Holy Land more times than he can count: "Israel is amazing, and I am so inspired, just being there. I feel at home. And during this journey I have become more and more engaged with politics, as well, and every time I see some fake news spread about Israel or when Israel is being bashed over something, I make sure to set it straight on my social media, and I don't care who reacts how to it, I am so proud to be a part of B'nei Israel."

Once the ceremony is over, I walk back to my hotel, taking the long way round, allowing myself almost an hour to wander the streets of Palermo. It's a city cut from an old-timey picture book, romantic and rustic with winding alleys and little old ladies arguing over the price of fish at the busy local market. I stop by a café and order a cappuccino, getting what I interpret as a dirty look for ordering a "morning coffee" beverage at 8:00 p.m. The sun is setting over the houses, making the entire city turn a pinkish hue, and for a moment, I'm falling in love with this place that broke the hearts of so many.

I visited the Inquisition prison on a Thursday morning, and the next day I prepare to sit down at a Shabbat table with people who had traveled much further than me. All of them have Jewish roots that were cut off during the Inquisition, but they have now chosen to return to their people and faith out of longing and conviction.

The gathering takes place in and old community center, where chairs have been set up to create a makeshift prayer room next to the dining hall where a group of women fill the tables with salads, bread, and bottles of wine. There are maybe twelve people in the room, most of them women, and once Rabbi Punturello starts leading the prayers, I notice that many of them don't have prayer books and are standing uncomfortably to the side. I offer the woman next to me my book and help her follow along in the words, and soon a group of women come up to us and we create a group-within-the-group, mixing prayers with a back and forth of questions and answers.

Two of the women are in the process of converting to Judaism, and the other two are just there as guests, curious about this new and exotic thing happening in their city. The two women are six months into their conversion studies, which were catalyzed by an article about the Italian *Marranos*—those forcibly converted during the inquisition. These women traced their own roots back to Jewish lineage. The decision to convert wasn't made easily; it took several meetings with the Rabbi and debates with family members that worried that a conversion would make it more difficult for them to find husbands and fit in socially, but once they joined the burgeoning community, they knew it was what they had to do.

"I know it sounds really silly and cliché, but from the first meeting with the group, it did feel like coming home. We all have quite similar stories and reasons for being here, and sharing this with the others feels kind of like gaining a family that helps me get through the tougher, more trying parts."

Clara is thirty-two, open and bubbly with a head of brown curls and modern, red-rimmed glasses, and she excitedly tells me that she has bonded with some of the other converts, especially the women. They get together socially now, and one of the most common topics of conversation is how to either find a nice Jewish husband or, if they're already married, how to make a marriage with a non-Jew work once they have converted. It's sweet to see her excitement, but it also strikes me as a naïve way of looking at a very complicated situation. Some of these women seem to have established lives with Christian husbands and will, assuming they finish their conversion, be forced to live observant lives separate from their spouses and children. Clara is single still, so for her the option of moving to Israel or an Italian city with a more robust Jewish life is still possible, but for others with more solid family ties to Palermo, this new life could prove to be incredibly challenging.

After prayers, the chairs are rearranged into a circle, and Rabbi Punturello gives a *shiur*, a short lecture on the week's Torah-portion. Although I don't really speak Italian, I can pick up the basic gist of what he is saying. The group is engaged and asks questions, especially one young man who I had heard praying loudly a bit earlier. His name is Sam, and he has taken to the classes with the perfect combination of enthusiasm and tenaciousness. I'm impressed by how much knowledge he has amassed in the thirteen months he has been coming here. Sam plans to move to Israel as soon as he has converted, and from what little I have seen of him, I have no doubt that he not only will do well, but that he was truly supposed to be here, doing this—re-joining the Jewish people.

While Sam hangs back with Rabbi Punturello, the rest of us take our seats around the table in the next room, and I'm seated between a sweet, elderly Jewish lady who lives just up the street and Michael Freund, the head of Shavei Israel, the Jerusalem-based organization that dedicates itself to helping "lost" Jews find their way back home. For Mr. Freund, this is a labor of love, and he has put significant time into fulfilling what he describes as a Zionist dream—helping Jews not only find their way home but also to connect them to the State of Israel, strengthening both the people and the place in the process.

Michael makes Kiddush, and when he's done, the room fills with friendly chatter in Italian while Rabbi Punturello helps with simultaneous translation for the English-speakers. From what I gather, most of these people are either undergoing or headed toward conversion, and one or two are Jewish by birth but somewhat estranged from the larger Jewish world. When I sit back and watch the group, hearing them sound out the words from the transliterated Jewish songbook, I wonder if the rejuvenated Jewish life in Palermo can grow into a sustainable community. Sam, the most active and involved member of this group, is likely to leave and start a family in Israel, and chances are Clara will as well. So where does that leave the Jewish revival of Palermo? What are the chances that this beautiful city will, once again, be a safe and thriving home for Jews?

Although I don't know the outcome of this story, I do know that I admire the work being done in Palermo, and I see the beauty of the redemptive event taking place, including this very dinner, just a stone's throw from the Palace of the Inquisition. Before coming to this meal, I had expected to feel sad given how few are in attendance, but instead I feel awe and pride and a hope, pure and uncensored for my otherwise-cynical character.

These are the descendants of those figures depicted in the murals on the walls of the Inquisition palace, a direct link to the pain I had felt as I ran my fingers along the etchings. They, if any, had deserved to bask in cynicism and bitterness, but instead they opted to live, and throughout the night I feel myself coming alive alongside them. These men and women are partaking in a ceremony of survivors, the answer to the question of how we are to remember those who were massacred and driven away. They are the promise and the lesson, so simply gathered around a table and in prayer.

As we finish dinner and start saying our goodbyes, I walk up to Clara, who is helping the other women clear the table. I hand Clara my prayer-book and tell her I want her to keep it, as a good-luck charm. Maybe it will even serve as a comfort and some encouragement in times of need. I'm not entirely sure why I did that, but Clara is thrilled and starts flipping through the pages, and I leave the building as she's still thanking me profusely. I don't know Clara, but I know I want her to do well, for the community to prosper and for old wounds to heal. In lieu of any actual guarantees, handing over that prayer-book feels like a desperate and impotent talisman intended to ensure all good things are to come.

Shabbat ends at 6:00 p.m. and not even an hour later, Angelo is waiting for me outside my hotel, leaned against his bright red Vespa. I laugh at the almost cartoonish sight: a bearded Italian man in an impeccable suit next to a Vespa, smilingly handing me an extra helmet. I climb on the back, thrilled to be living this Jewish version of a *Roman Holiday*. Palermo isn't Rome, I soon realize, and a Vespa is no place for a woman in a dress, so when we finally get to the night-open market, I am as grateful for having survived as I am for having kept my dignity intact.

The market is bustling, even at this hour, and Angelo takes me from store to store, picking out cheeses and cakes that have been kosher certificated by the local Rabbi. He is obviously in his element, and an hour into it, my backpack is filled to the brim with pickled anchovies, fruitcakes, and a variety of local cheese. Once I have more than I can carry, we find a café that provides much-needed sustenance in the form of biscotti and espresso. When I tell Angelo about my hopes and fears regarding the future of this burgeoning community and ask him how he sees his own future, he tells me that he travels a lot for work, and therefore is luckier than most.

"I go back and forth to London for work, and when I go there, I buy my kosher meat, I spend time with other Jews and get a sense of community that I can't really get here. That keeps me going, it helps me to keep kosher, and it definitely helps me meet Jews in a relaxed way."

I can read between the lines that he, at least partially, is referring to dating—something that must definitely be difficult in Palermo and even in Sicily as a whole, assuming you want to find a Jewish partner. For many of the people I met during that Shabbat dinner, this will be one of the biggest challenges: making sure that they can build a Jewish home here and not getting stuck standing on its fresh foundation facing myriad difficult choices. For Angelo, the decision has been made, and he is committed to his Jewish life. He strives to become more observant.

"If I lived in London full-time, I would be much more religious, of course, but it's not as easy as that. If Palermo didn't have this painful history, I probably wouldn't have felt compelled to come back to my people, and this place is in my blood, for better or worse. I am doing my best here, and my best here may be a lot more impactful than being the perfect Jew in London."

And he might be right.

Maybe this ancient community can rebuild on the shoulders of the few, the passionate and insistent, and carry on this legacy with dignity. Knowing how many slipped into the darkness of the Inquisition, the few may ultimately lead to the many, as more people are compelled to find their roots and return to Judaism. But that is, of course, the hopeful prognosis. The most realistic one is that, unless this community reaches a critical mass and sustains it, there is little hope for the Jews of Palermo long-term. Much has happened in the past five years, but it's one thing for the city and the region to invest in Jewish sites and tourism. Making it possible for Jews to live Jewish lives is another.

Regardless of the uphill battle, Angelo, Clara, and the others remain hopeful, encouraged by an engaged and dependable rabbi and organizations like Shavei taking an interest in their future and urging local leaders to do the same. They're on a mission of return, connected and motivated by the darkest parts of history.

The Jews of Palermo are standing at a crossroads to either become a memorial plaque or make a glorious return, but whatever the outcome, their journey is worth our admiration. The easy choice would have been to let things lie, to let the henchmen of the Inquisition win, but the returners of Palermo chose differently.

VENEZUELA

This chapter won't really be like the others. It came about in strange ways and ended up being perhaps the most meaningful Jewish experience I have ever had. I went to Venezuela to follow a revolution, but I came home with a new sense of belonging and a new closeness to the Jewish State.

But I'm getting ahead of myself; let me start from the very beginning.

For over twenty years, Venezuela has been on a steady and heartbreaking decline politically, societally, and economically. After Hugo Chávez got elected president in 1998, he swiftly began deconstructing the democratic and judiciary systems, and he implemented socialist policies that would take this once-wealthy nation to the bottom of every list. Despite having bigger oil resources than both Norway and Saudi Arabia, Venezuela fell apart, piece-by-piece and bit-by-bit. Both investors and the educated and able left the country, resulting in a swift fifteen percent loss of population and a halt to foreign investments. At first, Chávez could be perceived as a successful socialist leader, despite so many choosing to flee and the international community broadly questioning his policies, because he had the money to live up to his many lofty promises and provide a safety net that cushioned his citizens' lives. But that was a dream that would soon result in a rude awakening.

Chávez ran out of money, and his immediate solution to that was to manipulate the national currency, a mad quick fix that would lead to hyperinflation to the tune of many million percent. The Bolivars were soon worth close to nothing, making a simple bottle of milk cost literal barrels full of cash, assuming the increasingly poor population could afford such a luxury. As the population got angrier and more desperate, Chávez realized he would need to clamp down on the public outrage, and so he started arming the criminal elements of the favelas—the poorer neighborhoods of Caracas. Providing arms, money, and an ideological home, Chávez bought himself a paramilitary army that would shut down any discontent as the situation throughout Caracas worsened.

And worsened it did. Venezuela went from wealth and democracy to humanitarian disaster and dictatorship in just over twenty years, and today, children are dying from curable diseases, as they cannot be reached by medicine of even the most basic kind. The Venezuelan currency is worthless, and eighty-five percent of the population is living beneath the official poverty line of three U.S. dollars a month. All that is offered as aid to a dying population is a small bag of groceries once a month and the constant propaganda messaging that everything is OK. The crime in Venezuela is rampant, Caracas being the second most dangerous city in the world, and the combination of unfathomable poverty, government corruption, and street gangs creating a shadow society has made many lose hope in not only the government but society as we know it.

Hugo Chávez died in 2013, and to many of his closest aides' surprise, he chose Nicolás Maduro, a former bus driver with limited political experience, to be his successor. By this time, the patina of ideology and veneer of democracy had both worn off, and under Maduro's rule these past six years, Venezuela has morphed into a full-blown totalitarian regime. There are no free elections, no free press, and the citizens are being held hostage with food and violence. Maduro supporters will be rewarded with much-needed extra bags of rice or beans whereas those who dare oppose him will be stripped of even more basic needs and potentially suffer even harsher consequences by the hands of one of Maduro's many extrajudicial police forces. Maduro has none of the ideological clout that Chávez did, and to make up for it, he has stepped up the brutality in order to keep the Venezuelan people in line.

And that is what makes what is happening in Venezuela right now all the more impressive. It started on January 11th of 2019, as Nicolás Maduro started his second presidential term after a highly disputed election and rioting and protesting broke out in some of the poorest neighborhoods of Caracas. The protests grew in numbers and were supported by an invigorated opposition, led by the head of National Assembly, Juan Guaidó, who harnessed the power of a desperate people and saw the potential of a movement long overdue. On January 23rd, as tens of thousands had gathered in Caracas, Guaidó took to the stage and declared himself interim president in accordance with the Venezuelan constitution and called for "dictator" Maduro to immediately resign.

And that is when I decided I had to go and see this for myself.

Arriving in Venezuela for the first time is a punch to the gut, as nothing can really prepare you for the human suffering on display here or the degree to which this country is in a free-fall. I spend my first day in Caracas walking around Petare, one of the worst slums in the city. The streets are filled with families picking food from the trash, eating it right there, desperately seeking sustenance. My eye is drawn to one young man with boils all over his legs, the skin overtaken by infection. He gnaws at an almost bare chicken bone while he looks around frantically, as if he is afraid someone would steal it from his hands.

My bodyguard, Salazar, is next to me at all times, eyeing the surroundings, and a few minutes into our walk, I see his arm extend to the right of me as he grabs a young man running straight at me. I start running and end up at a square, standing next to a big statue of the national hero, Simón Bolívar. Behind it, there are colorful houses in rows up the steep mountain, structures that are hanging on by a thread. On many of them, there are paintings of Maduro and Hugo Chávez— scattered shards of a shattered dream.

Salazar catches up to me and explains that the man is a neighborhood watchman, a member of one of the criminal gangs Chávez put on the government payroll to police citizens as the country started to fall into chaos. Chávez provided money and weapons, and now, as Venezuela comes apart at the seams, these gangs have created a society within a society, combining a criminal enterprises of drugs, prostitution, and theft with their allegiance to the state. Police rarely come to the areas controlled by the neighborhood guerrillas, and the last line of public transport stops several miles away. Though the gangs have remained on the government's payroll, they are now less employees than freelance enforcers with no particular loyalty.

Although the guerrillas may be an extreme example, the concept of each man for himself has replaced the socialist agenda of solidarity all over Venezuela, as each citizen tries desperately to survive despite lawlessness, starvation, and unbridled corruption. The hospitals lack even the most basic supplies, and last month, Salazar tells me, five newborn infants died in the maternity ward from infections caused by the unsanitary conditions. In any other country, he says, there would be outrage and accountability, but here in Venezuela, there is silence. No media to cover it, no expectation of repercussions for the people who brought this on.

That culture of silence has created a strange and eerie mood here in Caracas, as the city is waiting for the next big clash following this month's protests and Juan Guaidó seeking to supplant Maduro as the legitimate president. One would expect that this crisis would have the city in an uproar, but it is a silent anger that fills the air, only to erupt in violence every other day before being squashed by government forces.

As I walk around the city, I see people going to and from work, waiting for the bus or chatting on a corner, but there are telltale signs of trouble if you know where to look. There are *"colectivos"*—a faction of violent and armed Maduro-loyalists—standing guard on every block, ready to pounce on protesters and journalists alike. Most shops and restaurants are boarded shut, the proprietors too frightened of riots to keep them open.

And they are right to be cautious; Maduro loyalists and opposition supporters plan to march through the city, both certain to bring protesters and pushback from the other side. The protests I have seen so far have all started peacefully and then suddenly shifted, as *colecti-vos*, government forces, and desperate citizens clash with an outcome as predictable as it is horrific. So far, there are three hundred confirmed dead and almost five thousand jailed as a result of the unrest, and the damage is, as most things in this socialist state, unevenly divided. Despite the odds, the people's opposition continues, and with every new protest, there are more flags, more people, and a little more hope that this will be the straw that breaks the camel's back.

Coming Home

On the fourth day, I go to the Jewish community, built around the Hebraica Jewish center in one of the nicer areas of downtown Caracas. I had been in contact with the Caracas Chabad family before coming, through the usual absurd-yet-familiar loops of Jewish connections, and the Rebbetzin had made a point of calling me before I left, urging me to reconsider: "I will pray every day that you find the wisdom not to come, but if you choose to go, I will help you in whatever way I can."

"That's Goldie," I realize that as soon as she meets up with me at the doors of the Chabad preschool. She is no-nonsense, loving and direct, and those are clearly necessary qualities when serving the Jews of Caracas. We do a walkthrough of the premises, and I am shocked by how vast it all is, a world inside a city: with schools, a bank, tennis courts, and restaurants.

There's a reason that they need this world. The Jews of Caracas have gone from thirty thousand to around six thousand in the past decade, as the national emergency has worsened. Targeted for kidnappings, their life here is highly structured and dependent on ever-present security measures, from bulletproof cars to a level of secrecy, and three young men I speak to give me a chillingly relaxed account of their circumstances.

"All three of us have been kidnapped. They grab you, ram your car or put a gun on you, and then keep you in one of those safe houses for a few hours while your family pays up. I know it sounds crazy, but it becomes less dramatic once you've lived with this threat for long enough. We call it the Caracas kidnap express."

The kidnappings are a profitable business here in Venezuela, many of them perpetrated by police officers who use their inside info to get addresses and access to potential victims, and the Jews are popular targets. Some of the remaining Jews here are, in fact, better off financially than non-Jewish Venezuelans but all are assumed to be, a classic stereotype that is far from unique to this country.

I am asked right away not to use any names or too many specifics when I write about the Jews here, and for this book, it's a first. Not even in Iran did I have to mask identities the way I will from now on, and that is just another part of the multi-layered complexity that is the Venezuelan Jewish community.

The Jewish community of Venezuela was officially established in the mid-nineteenth century, but there is evidence of a strong *Marrano* presence here much earlier, records speaking of forced baptism of Jews in the cities of Caracas and Maracaibo in the seventeenth century. Once the community started growing, it became the eclectic yet cohesive mass it is today, an even mix of Sephardi and Ashkenazi Jews who have bonded over a common hardship and, somewhat surprisingly, a common love for their Venezuelan homeland that has put them through so much.

I am asked to leave my security detail behind when I go to visit the Jewish center, and as soon as I enter, I can see that I don't need them. For the first time since I got to Venezuela, my shoulders relax, and I stop surveying my surroundings. This is a safe place, I can tell, and wherever I go there are signs that I have come home; from the old men in *kippot* having coffee and a game of backgammon by the pool to a group of kindergarteners running wild on the monkey bars. At Hebraica you don't have to worry about who you can trust or what lurks around the corner—the ones watching over you are your own. There are Israeli flags everywhere, an unequivocal statement of support for the Jewish state. The relationship between the state of Israel and the government of Venezuela may be in shambles, but the bond between Venezuelan Jews and their ancestral home is strong and undeniable. Most of the children here will end up going on at least one trip to Israel while they're at school, and many speak conversational Hebrew as a result of the ambitious curriculum. There's a mix of the religious and secular in the education here at Hebraica as well as in the community as a whole, but both sides get along and understand one's need for the other. There doesn't seem to be an us and them, but just a cohesive *we*, standing firm against the threats of the outside society.

I get the full tour, and then I am told that I am wanted upstairs for a short conversation. I don't know what that means, but I accept the invitation. As soon as I open the metal door to the third floor, I know what it's all about.

I have seen a lot of security personnel in my life through the destinations I choose to travel to and the line of work I am in. Many of them fill me with dread, some of them make me feel safe, but none have ever made me smile the way the Hebraica security did when I walked in that door.

"I hear you're doing some exciting stuff here in Venezuela."

The tall, blondish man is speaking in a distinct Hebrew accent and I laugh at his dry sarcasm.

"Yes," I tell him, "I heard that you're slacking off here in Caracas, so I thought I would give you guys something to do."

What happens next is both a blur and as clear as day. I am given a list of safety measures, emergency numbers, and general advice for my journalistic work in a country I, quite honestly, know very little about. I find myself apologizing for putting the Jewish community in this position, for placing them in the middle of a risky situation that I alone have assumed and accepted, but the man with the wry smile just shrugs and says, "We are family, and this is what we do."

Maybe you had to have been there to understand how deeply moving that moment was to me, or the sense of immediate relief I felt.

I had left Sweden for Venezuela—a country teetering on civil war—on impulse and without much preparation. I expected to be in it alone, to fight it all out and face the consequences, and here I found out that I had family that provided me a safe haven, should I ever need it.

The conversation lasts for about an hour, and even though I am unable to recount it in full, I will never forget the last thing said to me as I shake the hands of the people who have my back, no matter what: "We are here to take care of you, just know that. You are never alone as long as we are here."

When I go back to the car to meet up with my security detail, I avoid any questions on why it took so long or what I had done there. The protection I was just offered goes both ways, and I carry that responsibility like the last drop of water: with awe, care and gratitude.

When I get back to the hotel, there's a bag waiting for me with the concierge, and before he even hands it to me I know what's in it; I can smell the *challah* from over a mile away. The Chabad rabbi has sent someone over with candles, Kiddush wine and three newly baked *challot*, and without even thinking, I laugh out loud at the sight of this bag full of comfort in one of the world's most dangerous places.

The Venezuelan people, beaten down by violence, poverty, and corruption, saw Guaidó stand up to Maduro and followed his lead, and with their loud and united outcry the world started to listen. Country after country recognized Juan Guaidó as the legitimate president of Venezuela—from the U.S. to Canada and the European Union—whereas Nicolás Maduro's allies—Russia, Iran, China and Turkey—are not only few but also politically fickle as international pressure mounts against him.

In the past two weeks that I have spent here in Venezuela, there has been a clear push from both opposition and government as the presidential standoff is reaching a crescendo. The protests are now weekly and growing, and while Maduro is clearly choosing to push a narrative of this being a staged coup by Western imperialists, Guaidó is focusing his efforts on the millions of dollars of humanitarian aid that is about to reach Venezuela's border and that has been stopped repeatedly by Maduro's government, pointing to it being proof of not only Maduro's despotism but also his utter indifference toward the suffering of his own people. It is a war of words that may shift into a war of arms, as the army is said to be considering signing an amnesty agreement with Guaidó that would allow them to shift sides and support the interim president, thus hammering in the final nail in Maduro's political coffin.

Maduro has also received an offer of amnesty, but he is showing no sign of leaving, causing many Venezuelans to worry that there may be a pushback coming from this dictator with very little left to lose. So far, Maduro has stayed relatively silent throughout this dramatic month of political and societal upheaval, but it seems clear to most that this chaos won't be quelled by his usual insistence on preserving the status quo.

Once the situation in Caracas heats up, I start realizing that my two weeks here won't be enough. Having come here on an assignment that has now dried up, I frantically start looking for options, new work, any way in which to stay a few more days. I turn to Twitter, where I ask my followers to spread the word and have anyone looking for a freelance contact me through private message. Not even ten minutes after I post the tweet, I hear that familiar ding and, in my inbox, there is a short message in Hebrew.

"Please send me your phone number, there are some people who want to help you."

Maybe I should have hesitated, but I didn't. It might have been the Hebrew or the simplicity of the sentence, but I sent the stranger my phone number, and, almost immediately thereafter, my phone rang.

"Hola, my name is Carlos, and I heard you might need some help."

His name is Carlos Cohen, and he is part of a large Jewish family who has lived in Caracas for over eighty years. His father emigrated from Tehran by way of Jerusalem, and today the family runs a highly successful business that operates in almost thirty cities around the entire country.

Through a divine intervention that I can't explain and hardly understand, it turns out that Carlos' family owns and operates the hotel I am staying in, and he graciously offers to cover my stay for as long as I want and to help out in any other way I need for as long as I decide to stay in Venezuela.

His call, offer, and the bizarre circumstances of this situation all astound me, but I don't have time to react, since as soon as we hang up, my phone rings again, and again, with other Jews who want to come to my aid. Somehow, I am now part of this chain of Venezuelan Jews—expats as well as remainers—and they all express their gratitude toward me for showing their country and its plight to the world.

I'm on the phone for about an hour, and by the end of it, I not only have six new friends but also an invitation to the Cohens for Shabbat. An hour, that's all it took, for me to go from being at my wits' end to having more solutions than I knew what to do with. I wasn't sure exactly how this happened, but I knew why, and the words of the Israeli security guy suddenly seemed like prophecy.

The next day, I head to the eighth floor of my hotel, where the Cohens have their offices. I am expecting to meet one of uncles for a quick cup of coffee, but then I get there, six people are waiting for me, all from different branches of the family. There's immediacy to them, beyond the normal South American kiss-on-cheek-and-hug culture. They're excited to see me, and right away, they want to see the photos from the adventures and show their own from what all seven of us think is the beginning of a revolution.

The Cohens have high hopes for Guaidó and tell me that he, at least privately, has good ties to the Jewish community and is willing to defrost relations to Israel as soon as Maduro is gone. A Guaidó presidency would mean an easier life for the Cohen family, as it would for most other Venezuelans; under Chávez and Maduro they have had to bite their tongue and walk a very perilous line in order to stay in business. Chávez took land from them more than once under the guise of appropriation for the good of the people, and in socialist Venezuela there are no lawsuits or measures to be done in order to seek justice. So, they grin and bear it and try to maintain bearable relationships to a government that fights them and their business at almost every turn.

The Cohens employ thousands of people, and their commitment to Venezuela is, if not surprising, then at least inspirational. Most of the family members are involved in some kind of social charity, most of which are at odds with the Maduro regime, and before I even finish my first cup of coffee, they invite me to visit one of their flagship projects, the Fundana orphanage in central Caracas.

Maduro's Shame

"Just this past month, we have taken in twenty-seven babies who were left in the street, newborns who had been left in a box by the side of the road, as were they yesterday's trash."

It's almost impossible to square her words with the sight before me—these innocent, beautiful babies whose cribs are lining the small room.

This private orphanage specializes in taking in children who have been abandoned by their mothers because they lack food and most other basic necessities. The babies are abandoned either right after birth, or they are simply dropped off somewhere on the street after the mother realizes she doesn't have the means to care for her children. Once the children reach Fundana, they are usually already on the brink of starvation, and many are suffering from drug withdrawal and disease that has been transported between mother and child due to non-existent prenatal healthcare.

It has gotten worse in the past few weeks, Karen, the head counselor, tells me. It used to be the case that Venezuela's social services managed the contact between the parents and Fundana, providing offices in the most destitute areas of Caracas where the babies could be dropped off safely, but since this latest political crisis started just over a month ago, Maduro's government has closed those offices down, trying to hide these families' suffering from the eyes of the world.

"There used to be a facility in Petare where mothers could leave their kids—a kind of halfway-house between them and us—but after the regime shut it down a few weeks ago, these mothers have nowhere to turn, and that means that these babies end up right on the street. Last week, a member of our team found a one-year-old, half-naked outside the subway with nothing [other] than a ragged old blanket to sit on and a single cookie, in a bag, tied to his wrist."

It is hard, if not impossible, to imagine. These children, 130 just at the Fundana orphanage, have been abandoned not just by their mothers but also by Maduro, by Venezuela, by everything that is good and pure in what we consider civilized society. These mothers have no other recourse, but the Venezuelan government does, yet time and time again it chooses ideology over humanity.

At Fundana they are doing as best they can with the resources the socialist government allows, but they lack basic necessities such as medicines, diapers, and formula—things they are forced to smuggle in from Miami or buy from the black market at massive costs. When I ask them if they have done public appeals for help, they say that they can't do that in national media, as too much spotlight on the humanitarian crisis would cause Maduro to shut down Fundana, and places like it, for good.

What's being done here is guerilla-style humanitarian work, while these babies' lives hang in the balance. There is no doubt in my mind that all of these children would be dead were it not for the work done by the women at Fundana, holding them, feeding them, clothing them, every day.

This is the most palpable piece of evidence of the Venezuelan crisis that I have seen during my two-week stay in the country and undoubtedly the most heartbreaking. Babies being left in the street because their mothers think that way, they will at least have a shot: a diffuse hope that someone, somewhere, will have mercy on them.

My eyes are drawn to this little girl with long, beautiful eyelashes and a few dark curls just on top of her little head. I lift her up, and she weighs close to nothing, despite her being almost a year old. When I look at her, I am met by eyes that have already seen far too much of the dark facets of life.

Her name is Rosa, and she is ten months old. When she was just a few hours old, her mother dropped her off outside Fundana, never to return. I can't let go of Rosa. I hold her in my arms while tears stream down my face, and all I want is to take her home and give her a life far away from all of this, to save her from the many trials that await this innocent, beautiful child.

It's a naïve thought, I know that, but after a few weeks here in Venezuela, I so desperately need to save one soul, make just one thing right, to get a happy ending to this heartbreaking story of corruption, abuse of power, and one evil regime's complete and utter indifference to human suffering.

But I can't save Rosa. I have nothing to offer this country that I have grown to love, against all odds. When I step outside Fundana's doors I feel, for the first time, a genuine hatred toward this regime and anyone who has helped build and sustain a myth that is now killing these children. This is genocide, no more and no less, and I see that now. Tens of thousands of children are dying in the name of socialism, and none of the proponents of this ideology have the decency to remember their names or visit their graves once they are sacrificed.

This is what remains of the Good Left's pet project: death, starvation, and unfathomable human suffering. That and nothing else is the legacy they chose.

I cry when I leave Rosa, and I am well aware of how impotent and useless those tears really are. She is one of many thousands, millions, who are suffering at the hands of the Maduro regime, but it was in her eyes that this crisis became flesh and blood for me.

These children are dying, and meanwhile, politicians and intellectuals around the world are still defending this regime and fighting those fighting it and what it stands for. I pray that one day, they will have the sense to hang their heads in shame as they see what I just saw: dying children, desperate mothers, and a country being robbed of hope and treasure.

We can never say that we didn't know, because we do. We can never pretend that this didn't happen, because we were there.

A Shabbat in the Middle of a Revolution

It isn't easy to square the misery I have encountered in the past few weeks with the opulence and beauty of the Cohen home. Placed snugly just beneath the gorgeous Ávila mountain, the vast Bauhaus structure is lit from the side, casting shadows across the private park, filling up with Cohen family members.

I feel somewhat out of place. I had packed for a week, but now, on my third week of this trip, my clothes and person have seen better days, and as I am stepping into perfection, I am acutely aware of the state of my one suitable dress and the mismatched red backpack slung across my shoulder. Everyone here looks perfect, and I look as if I am the exotic guest, an odd curiosity that walked in from the streets of a place best not visited.

I'm greeted by smiles and hugs from over forty people, and they all reiterate the same thing: that I have family in Caracas now, and whatever I need, whenever I need it, they are here for me. I slowly get more comfortable, and when one of the young sons from one of the branches—I'm not sure which—makes Kiddush, I am blessed to be able to fully appreciate the moment. The word *magical* is shamelessly overused, but here, it fits—here, it is the only fitting adjective. We are in the middle of a revolution, and we say these ancient words out into the jungle and celebrate our mutual heritage among strangers, family. and friends.

"Maduuuuurooooo!" The matriarch yells out, all of a sudden.

"Coño e tu madre!" The crowd replies, and we all erupt in laughter.

The "Maduro challenge"—yelling out the dictator's name and responding with "is a motherfucker"—has become a viral sensation. It may seem like a childish game, but for the people of Venezuela it is a sign of a burgeoning freedom, a rare expression of free speech in a country where silence has been the rule of law for over two decades.

The community here in Venezuela is deeply traditional but not necessarily religious, despite having the resources for observance. According to the Chabad rabbi, many of them keep kosher to some extent, but few are *shomer* Shabbat or go to synagogue regularly. Shabbat, however, is a constant, and the connection between the Jews is indivisible. The Jews here—regardless of observance level and social status—are family, and they look out for each other. Despite the Jewish education here being private and associated with some costs, there are exemptions for those who can't afford tuition, and no Jewish child is denied a spot at the

Jewish school or any of the Jewish activities offered at Hebraica. The crisis, now going on twenty-one years, has focused this community, and they don't have the luxury of infighting or sectarianism. Here, a Jew is a Jew is a Jew. And a Jew is family.

The dinner discussion is dominated by politics, and everyone there wants to offer their opinion on what is about to happen and ask me mine, and we debate the threat of civil war while digging into some of the best food I have ever had. It's absurd and wonderful, like accessing two worlds at once, but I seem to be the only one who reacts to the bizarre juxtaposition. The Jews of Venezuela are used to inhabiting many different universes, and they have learned to do so with ease, without fighting the socialist machine but rather understanding its cogs and knowing when to push and when to let go.

"You see why we don't want to leave, right?" Talma, one of the matriarchs, sits down at my table and nods to the crowd, laughing and singing on the surrounding greens. "In a way, we have everything, even with the troubles, and we truly love this country; it is more than our home—it is our heart."

And yes, I do get it. Venezuela has a way of capturing your heart and making you love it, despite the trials it puts you through. There is magic here, and more importantly, an untapped potential, and every Venezuelan in- and outside its borders is waiting impatiently for it to be released.

A Watched Pot

It's a strange thing, waiting for a revolution, because there is a lull that sets in amid the chaos. I get used to the shootings outside my hotel and even wearing the uncomfortable bulletproof vest; this is life in Venezuela as we know it.

What does surprise me are the rumors that start swirling about my presence in the country, starting in Arab media and trickling down to my colleagues on the ground, and eventually reaching me. On the twelfth day of my trip, a colleague from the Algerian media comes up to me and asks me to my face if I'm an Israeli spy, and when I laugh, his face doesn't even register a reaction.

"You can tell me. I will understand, but you have to tell me."

It's not that this hasn't happened before; as a Jewish woman traveling around to some of the world's most dangerous places, I have been subjected to these accusations numerous times. But the intensity of the accusations is different here. Both Chávez and Maduro have marinated this society in anti-Semitism and conspiracy theories involving Israel and America and the threat of an imperialist coup, and now that the government is threatened, it is ramping up the anti-Jewish and anti-Western propaganda.

For the first time since getting to Venezuela, I feel personally threatened. Knowing that I am a journalist without a visa in a country involved in a low-level civil war I could handle, but knowing that the government looking for an excuse to detain reporters may now have found a perfect fit really rattles me.

I can feel a growing distance between me and my colleagues from the Arab media staying at the same hotel, and the silence that fills the room as soon as I enter. I feel lonely in Caracas, suddenly, until I remember the words from a couple of weeks ago:

"We are here to take care of you; just know that. You are never alone as long as we are here."

So I call the number I was given, and I reach out to my family.

It's a short call, but it's enough, as often is the case with family. The reassurances, the unconditional backup, it gives you what you need to face the world again. It's funny. I went to this country so far from home, and not only did I find family, but what saved me, what had my back and guaranteed my safety, was the State of Israel.

My last week in Venezuela is spent more on my toes but with a newfound calm, keeping myself to myself while reporting from a country in turmoil. On my last day, there's another big opposition rally, and when I head into the six hundred thousand-person crowd, I pray that this will be the last big push we've all been waiting for.

But it isn't. Despite the masses, Guaidó's inspirational speech and the built-up tension releasing across Caracas, there is still a ways to go, and I leave the square both uplifted and disappointed.

I wanted to come here for a revolution; I desperately hoped that I would get to see the world change. What I experienced was something much more complicated, heartbreaking, and beautiful.

I had less contact with the organized Jewish community in Venezuela than I usually do during these trips, but it ended up being one of the most meaningful Jewish experiences I have ever had. After having written about Jewish continuity, peoplehood, and solidarity for almost two years, I got to see it in action in a very real way. I called out and they came for me; I needed them and they aided me; they were my home when I was lost in no man's land.

Of all the places I expected to find the answers to my initial question—why do we survive as a people—Venezuela would have been one of the last. But here, I got it in the simplest and most beautiful of ways. We survive because we come for each other, we aid each other, and we are each other's home when there is no other.

I leave Venezuela after a little more than three weeks, knowing I will be back, sooner rather than later. Not just for the revolution, this time, but also for a family reunion, with all of those who now fill my heart and my WhatsApp feed after the adventure of a lifetime.

An Ever-Dying People?

"A people dying for thousands of years means a living people. Our incessant dying means uninterrupted living, rising, standing up, beginning anew... If we are the last, let us be the last as our fathers and forefathers were. Let us prepare the ground for the last Jews who will come after us, and for the last Jews who will rise after them, and so on until the end of days."

—Simon Rawidowicz

When I was a girl, before I left the house, my mother would always say that I should take a jacket for the cold and a passport for the persecution. It slipped out of her mouth effortlessly, like an "I love you" or a "see you soon," but the greeting was an internalization of a lesson that has shaped our people throughout time. We Jews have seen few years without peril and persecution, to the extent that it is engrained in our common identity, shaping our thoughts and behavior. We have been dying since 587 BCE and have survived for just as long, and in that tension lay a mystery I knew would be worth exploring.

These stories from the Diaspora are snapshots, of course, but they are also an attempt at finding out how these remaining Jewish communities have survived throughout the ages; what facilitated their ability to remain distinctly Jewish; and what it is within our people, faith and culture that ensures not only our survival but our prosperity in the face of such adversity. The goal was to understand how these vestiges of Jewish life, culture, and people have survived and retained their distinctly Jewish identity in lands that have sought to extinguish them. What started as an almost academic study became a journey into the radically unknown and comfortably familiar: being a Jew among Jews in places I had never visited. To call it a profound experience would be an understatement.

After nearly two years, more than a dozen countries, and hundreds of interviews, I cannot claim to have solved the mystery of Jewish survival, but I have been able to draw a few conclusions to answer those initial questions:

- *Orthodox communities fare much better than their conservative or progressive counterparts.*

The communities that adhere to orthodox practices are naturally protected against assimilation and intermarriage, and through that, they are more likely to secure a Jewish lineage for future generations.

- *A larger community is not necessarily more vibrant and viable.*

For example, Sweden, with its fifteen thousand Jews, is in many ways less viable than neighboring Finland with a mere fifteen hundred, and the small community of Djerba will most likely have a stronger Jewish base in a hundred years than the much larger Uzbek community. A large community can be lulled into a false sense of security, leaving the responsibility of Jewish life to someone else. Whereas smaller communities can have a sense of urgency and are more likely to band together, turning their Jewish observance into an act of rebellion and survival.

- *Religion begets religion.*

The Jewish communities that exist in highly secular societies (Sweden, Cuba, Uzbekistan) tend to lose their religion, whereas communities in very religious societies remain traditional and observant. One might think that it would be easier for Jews to live alongside atheists than religious Muslims, but from what I have found during these travels, religious neighbors help promote Jewish observance and continuity and create a society where expressions of religious identity are natural and commonplace.

- *A level of isolation often benefits Jewish communities.*

The communities that have returned, at least in some form, to the shtetl-life are both stronger and less vulnerable than those that try to mix and intermingle with the majority population. Djerba is the most remarkable example of this, where roughly fifteen hundred Jews live in their own part of the island and actively choose not to mix with non-Jews socially. Some of these communities are isolated by others and not by choice, but the result is the same: a homogenous society that contains its culture and values. When the Jews attempt to actively intermingle and adapt, the cultural exchange seems to only go one way—Jews adapting to the majority religion and culture and not the other way around—inevitably blurring the line between integration and assimilation.

- *Diaspora Jews are connected to Israel...*

Even in countries where the Jews are prohibited from expressing solidarity with the state of Israel, the bond with the *land* of Israel is immensely strong, Iran being the most extraordinary example. Without minimizing the obvious issues with totalitarian regime's policies of differentiating between Jews and their ancestral land as a Jewish state, one can see the benefits of a community relating to and bonding around the land of Israel on a strictly religious level.

- *...But that relationship is complicated.*

The relationship with Israel is not entirely uncomplicated for Diaspora Jews and has facets of which major Jewish communities in the United States and Europe are unaware. In Djerba, for instance, the Jews chose not to make Aliyah out of fear of becoming secular. In several other countries, there was clear upset over what the Jewish community perceived as pressure to leave their place in the world and join the larger Israeli community. The "Israel issue" has become a divisive one for much of the Diaspora, the conflict stemming from a feeling of being either ignored entirely or used as a sound bite, and that the unique cultural expressions of these communities are not being respected or valued.

- *Holocaust remembrance has both a push and pull effect on Jewish identity.*

In communities where one relies too heavily on Holocaust remembrance as an expression of Jewish identity, such as in Sweden, it has replaced religion and observance. In others, such as Morocco, the remembrance is closely tied to tradition and faith. The third option, as seen in Uzbekistan and Finland, the Jews identify as soldiers, banding together with their non-Jewish brothers to fight a common enemy rather than being victims of both. Holocaust remembrance in those communities has a very different emphasis, not unlike Yom HaShoah in Israel, where resistance shares equal billing with victimization. In communities where there is very little organized Holocaust remembrance, such as Iran and Tunisia, it seems to not have affected the Jewish identity to any large extent. Despite it being somewhat taboo, there is reason to suggest that a relationship to the Holocaust isn't a factor in Jewish survival, but that Holocaust remembrance as a replacement for identity is.

Challenges Ahead

The history of the diaspora can and must be divided into before and after the birth of the State of Israel. Before 1948, we Jews related to the dream, and now we relate to the reality, and as in many relationships, the tangible reality is far more contentious and complex than the idealistic dream. As Israel grows stronger and the Diaspora is suffering threats from both without and within, the power balance has irreversibly shifted and put the Jewish state in a position where it must make its mind up about the rest of the Jewish world.

Either the State of Israel makes the survival of the Diaspora a priority or gears any efforts toward encouraging Aliyah, and it seems that—at least for now—they have their hearts set on the latter.

In December of 2018, Naftali Bennett, head of the Education and Diaspora ministries in Benjamin Netanyahu's government, gave a statement about what he views as a Diaspora in crisis.: "We're used to being told that it's because of prayer rules at the Western Wall, the Palestinian issue, and other ideological controversies. It's not correct. There is a problem of serious assimilation, and a growing apathy among Jews in the Diaspora, both about their Jewish identity and their connection to Israel. That's the key story, and it's a national challenge."

The statement isn't necessarily untrue, but the fact that it was made during an Aliyah-push where the Israeli government is actively encouraging French Jews to relocate to Israel, does give several clues as to why there has been a breakdown in communication between Israel and the Diaspora, and why the hurt feelings among Diaspora Jews may not be entirely unwarranted. On the one hand, we have the State of Israel urging Diaspora Jews to come home; on the other, Diaspora Jews are asking the Jewish State to acknowledge and protect the only home they've ever known, preserving millennia of history and culture in the process. The relationship to Israel has been turned into a binary choice—a yes or no option—and the more you see of the Diaspora, the more you realize that the reality is far too complicated for such a black-or-white approach.

If Israel wants to actively help the Diaspora survive, efforts could be made to if not ensure then at least aid its survival, by focusing on Jewish education from religious literacy to Hebrew studies, and offering direct legal and diplomatic aid to communities that are fighting anti-Jewish legislation. Assuming these observations are applicable in a larger context, a more observant Diaspora is a stronger Diaspora, and many communities today are lacking the infrastructure for that observance, such as access to kosher food, a community rabbi, or a communal space in which to gather. If the survival of the Diaspora matters, and that may be a big "if" in this debate, then its observance must matter, as well. I would be remiss if, when discussing these issues, I didn't recognize the tremendous work done by Chabad-Lubavitch. This New York-based Hasidic organization has existed in its modern form since the 1940s, and today it has emissaries in over one hundred countries around the world, being the only vestiges of Jewish life in many remote communities around the world. The controversy surrounding Chabad is that their emissaries come and replace the original Jewish expressions and observances in communities with their own strain of Judaism, and that argument has merit. But as of now, there are no other entities attempting to offer an alternative. The ideal would be for these communities to be supported so that they can preserve their own specific Jewish culture, but up and until that happens, Chabad are helping many Jews stay Jewish, tirelessly and often without thanks.

Apart from the relationship with Israel, the Diaspora faces a multi-faceted challenge, from the perennial anti-Semitism and its modern incarnation of radical Islam to the downfall of Western civilization and the attack on the values that make up the foundation of Jewish ethics and thought. We are no longer in a position of "just" having to defend Jewish lives against overt aggression but also the very ideas of religious observance, tradition, family, and adherence to a code of ethics against a cultural warfare that is equally, if not more, lethal.

As I set out to research this book, people asked me if this work would be a defense of the Diaspora, its validity and future. The truth is, it was never supposed to be, but the more I saw of this Jewish world, the more I realized its worth to all of us, Jews and non-Jews alike.

The variety of Jewish expression, from Iran to Irkutsk, has developed since the Babylonian exile and is breathing and growing to this day. To value that and even accept that there are two parallel Jewish worlds—inside and outside of Israel—is not to deny or minimize the bond between a people and their land but to value the Jewish experience, wherever it takes place and to defend a Jew's right to settle anywhere— freely and safely.

Jews are sometimes called the canary in the coalmine of Western civilization, but after seeing what I've seen over the past few years I would add that the Jewish Diaspora is the last line of defense against a world whose grasp of what matters is increasingly diminishing. The canary connotes inaction, simply reacting to events around it, but Jews across the world are anything but passive. They are fighting to preserve thousands of years of values and faith, constantly moving against the grain, and that must be worth protecting. The fight these communities are engaged in—trying to stay Jewish against all odds—is a fight that should be supported by anyone who cares about the future of the West and who shares the values that are lost with every Jewish community that perishes.

I carry my passport with me wherever I go, and I have ever since I was little. Not because I have always felt under direct threat, but because that is part of my Diaspora identity, a kneejerk reaction, an ever-present wordless prayer. Given my leeriness, one would think the choice to make Aliyah—to move to Israel—would be a simple one, but as many other diaspora Jews know, my heart has more than one home, and my Jewish identity and expression is a result of my history. They are the miracles and strife that I carry with me, proudly. The people I met around the world for the past eighteen months have that same dual identity and the same pride and, much like me, they want their identity and history to matter to the rest of the Jewish world. We are more than the last ones left at the party; we are survivors, the strongest of the lot.

"Eighty years ago, we were shards of glass, trampled and bleeding on the ground. Today, we are diamonds, scattered across the world."

An elderly Siberian man uttered these words inside a colorful synagogue in Irkutsk, after I had asked him what it meant to be a Jew in the Diaspora. His words resonate with me because he captured not only the hardship but also the beauty of *us*, of how pressure turned us into diamonds to glimmer unto the nations. That is not the description of victimhood, but of peoplehood, and that is at the heart of what and who we are.

Despite all the challenges I have described and related, I have never felt more hopeful about the Jewish world than I do after seeing so much of it, because there is one thing that didn't make it onto my list—a key to Jewish survival that isn't quantifiable or rational, at all—we are a miracle, our existence defies belief, and the fact that we survived while seeing mighty empires fall around us fills even the most cynical with faith, resilience, and hope. We come in all colors, exist in every corner of the world and, with us, carry all its vast memory. We are ancient beings in a modern world. Should the Diaspora die, these memories will die with us, as will the ancient expressions of tradition that we fought so hard to uphold. That would undoubtedly be a tragedy. Not just for us, but for the world, and to anyone who believes in the value of believers.

So, if we are the last, let us be the last as our fathers and forefathers were. Let us prepare the ground for the last Jews who will come after us, and for the last Jews who will rise after them, and so on until the end of days.

ACKNOWLEDGMENTS

I have dreamt of writing this book ever since I was a little girl, but back then, I didn't realize just how much of a village it takes to make one woman's dream come true. I owe so many people a great debt of gratitude for their help, encouragement and—when I needed it—scoldings and kicks to the backside.

To Aylana Meisel, who pushed and helped and listened on my best and worst days, I am forever grateful for your friendship and guidance.

To Anna Ask, my BFF and sister soldier, for putting up with me and making me laugh through the tears. I love you, and I thank you.

To my Adat Jeshurun family. You are my home, my people, and wherever I go I return to you.

To Neil Kozodoy for taking a chance on me way back when and always being around for good advice, encouragement, and the best editing in the business.

To Tiffany Gabbay for her hard work and dedication, making this dream come true when I thought it wouldn't.

To David S. Bernstein and everyone at Bombardier Books for believing in me and this book.

To Elisabet and her family for true friendship and safe spaces.

To the Tikvah Fund for its support and guidance.

ACKNOWLEDGMENTS

To Michael Freund and Shavei Israel for his incredible work and undying dedication to the Jewish people—none of this would have been possible without you.

To Rabbi and Rebbetzen Greisman and Chabad for providing spiritual and physical homes for me and many others across the globe.

To everyone else who did me kindnesses throughout these two years—thank you. I will do my very best to repay the debt.

Finally, I would like to thank all of my Jewish brothers and sisters who shared their homes, tables, stories, and lives with me throughout this process. This book belongs to all of them, along with a piece of my heart, left behind in every city and country I was lucky enough to visit. I hope I did all of you justice; any errors and faults are mine.

ENDNOTES

1 Hernroth-Rothstein, Annika, "The Silent Scream of Iran's Jews," *The Tower Magazine*, Issue 42, September 2016, http://www.thetower.org/article/the-silent-scream-of-irans-jews/.

2 Hernroth-Rothstein, Annika, "Totalitarian Terror in Tehran," *The Tower Magazine*, Issue 38, May 2016, http://www.thetower.org/article/totalitarian-terror-in-tehran/.

3 Hernroth-Rothstein, Annika, "'We Don't Want to Forget': In Tehran, Revenge is a National Ethos," *The Tower Magazine*, Issue 39, June 2016, http://www.thetower.org/article/we-dont-want-to-forget-in-tehran-revenge-is-a-national-ethos/.